MIND POWER IS MONEY

MIND POWER IS MONEY

EDRIC ETTIENNE

MIND POWER IS MONEY

iUniverse books may be ordered through booksellers or by contacting:

iUniverse
1663 Liberty Drive
Bloomington, IN 47403
www.iuniverse.com
1-800-Authors (1-800-288-4677)

ISBN: 978-1-5320-4247-8 (sc)
ISBN: 978-1-5320-4248-5 (e)

Library of Congress Control Number: 2018902364

Print information available on the last page.

iUniverse rev. date: 02/21/2018

These are my original lines authentic like a heartbeat [oops] I made a starting blunder what I claimed to be mines is owned by the mind. The act of a powerful mind is to inform and edify; as power comes from within without any warning, we were all retro fitted in the beginning regardless of our circumstances this is my flow, so let's put on a show. The art of wording starts with the Word itself' we rely on the word for expression and satisfaction; our participation makes this a special occasion, without this action we would be like mummies' talking loud but saying nothing money though is an automatic safety net; that catches many in its net, as it is mobile power' it is an instant makeover which has the potential to devour or to favor. While researching for this project I was set straight by the mind as I never gave it the credit that it deserved, I always had the brain up there and the mind down here' but I know better now.

Human intentions are good for the most part; but when you get locked in the money cage it changes us at every stage' welcome to the assimilation phase.

This is my inner light shining out; to shine on those whose light is dimmed out.

This is me popping up like a bubble after simmering and not expecting; the genie got out and there is no way to shot him out.

I have been tried and tested now I am aware of myself; I was convinced I did not have the pedigree; but I was judging myself in the wrong category.

Being schooled in the society of hard knocks every turn was another knock, so if you venture somewhere and you don't get knock down right away' at least you are prepared for the crash that could hit you like whip lash. My credentials are fundamental basic and hypnotic, they always remain the same so they have been instrumental in keeping me grounded' keeping it simple is what I do without much trouble; these days the masses seek sophistication, that is like running into trouble in a can, simplicity is the ultimate form of sophistication' I do not know if the learned could get that; being teacher proof don't resolve you from existing proof; I am just a salmon swimming upstream blowing off some steam.

Take a chance on this rookie writer, I am a straight shooter and practicing sniper, my weapon of choice is my words you might be pleasantly surprised if you hop on for the ride, there is a power in words and I love to pull the trigger; this is a perspective from a have not' about your typical have newt's, as everything is about the have's or those who have, as we all strive to have' our life long struggle is just too have, welcome to the try' why not try, I see it as the survival commandment' this is my try.

I am swamped with words, I don't lack for words' I am ready to vent and I promise not to invent, I don't want to drain the swamp, as I might have to indulge the swamp' as that is where the incumbents reside, like those writers who are already inside' getting in the door will be interesting. I want to show that I deserve an invite when the time is right' this is my launch void of fanfare on this tourer fare, I will do what is expedient and keep it real as a form of convenience' it is all a learning experience of consequences, as we live we must learn or it would be to our detriment. I have discovered that money possesses me like an evil spirit and it manipulates me, trying to avoid it has so far been futile' is it just me or is it every body, I try to act tough, but without money things are rough, I could bluff about stuff' but sooner or later I will have to call my bluff and face up, reality is money is transitional and a go to option.

Life is an act and that's a fact' it will serve us good to remember that.

We are all actors trying to make sense of our actions, but not many of us realize that, it's just that some are paid and most of us are unpaid' but we play the same game again and again, although it differs from stage to stage, to get by on a daily basis we need to act' even if we don't know we need to act like we know' a flaw in society that is accepted unconditionally, one cannot be skeptical as actions speaks louder than words.

Everybody know there is always someone waiting to show and glow, so while winging it we got to bring it, everybody got to wing it sometimes' as you got to bring it all the time, nothing is wrong in wanting to be somebody known; because when you want to be' you will make that extra effort if only for taught comfort.

The try is one of the ways to level the playing field; as when you try out you could find out, we are all boxed in some sort of way as the system of manipulation dictates for us; but if we dare to detour on the side it could be life changing, but we must disrupt our comfort zone in order to get into a new zone' thinking outside the box is a must, like the early bird catches the worm; you need to be ready to conquer, the fruit is ready for the picking somebody has to do the picking why not me or why not you; too few takes up the challenge preferring to not take a stance, excuses are a dime a dozen do not let them bury you in there prison' different clerks are to take you because you are free, as everybody loves a freebee and a free ride' being a jockey and riding somebody comes naturally to everybody, as long as you allow someone to ride you they will continue to so do; as we teach others how to treat us by not speaking up' no should not mean yes and yes should not mean no for sure. Settling is a two way street but most of us use it to retreat, not wanting to be confrontational and rock the boat, but order comes from chaos and chaos comes from order; whenever either is challenged we get a new order.

As something new is always welcomed by the masses; as so few is volunteered by leaches, so if settling is your plan it must be part of your game plan.

Settling does not have to be giving in; it could be temporary and work out like a complementary, as a strategy could be introduced very easily.

As long as the game is being played' strategies are fair gain just an edge could give you the cutting edge.

That edge could be a hunch with it you could eat somebody lunch; an edge could be like a sliver to slightly derail to no avail.

Like when change happens it is so minuscule it seems unlikely to change the rules.

That is how it is overlooked before you know it the claim has been made.

As the validation has already been made; reversal has been replaced with refusal, making it seem unnatural.

Going back is usually marred by obstacles impeding progress because the stuff has already been set; like a moment in time is already set in stone so it is better left alone. All this time the mind has been playing an integral part from the start; just hint it then the mind will run with it' just look at how comfortable the mind makes you feel with virtual reality, clearing the way for different realities. Mind power is on the money; it could take you for a ride without money, it is closer to the lord than any amount of money' harness the mind and you on the money.

A good teacher and a good follower is the mind of course.

What does gives you sharp intellect the brain off course, but the brain cannot contain the mind as the brain is tangible and the mind is intangible.

One is physical referring to the brain and the other is mental referring to the mind; as the physical form is no match for the mental' the brain cannot contain the mind, like air on its own the mind works fine and the mind maintains the brain, so brain power does not exist without mind power.

So the powerful brain still need an assist orchestrated by the mind; Endurance and perseverance is often accredited to the mind' that stick to it sens and staying power are attributes of the mind; the brain could waver but the mind is a stayer' count on the mind to carry you and to stand by you for true; the brain could fail you as it is a muscle, if you do not use it chances are you can lose it; the mind is there for the long hall, as mental is permanent. The concept of spirituality is limited from the standpoint of the brain. But when we implore the mind the connection gets deeper.

Even if we become a sleeper; it is slow and steady marathon like. Not exerting too much energy but being focused; one pointed is the method to the madness. Getting it done getting anything done starts with baby steps; as confidence grows then it starts to show. In the beginning things look so promising' the feeling is anything could be accomplished, but how we end up is what chokes us up. As we never see what is coming while we are running life.

Dealing with strife is like handling a sharpened knife; focusing keeps right. The desired goal is surviving and continuing to do some accomplishing. Life is a movie and our scripts are fixed and getting out of it is a myth.

We are predestined to get our fix as we are per equipped with blinders. But our hands are free, if we remove our blinders we might be able to multitask; our brain and mind power are testaments to that fact. As only those of us who dare to remove there blinders; to get in touch with themselves are going to be able to find themselves.

You must know yourself before you could successfully manipulate money. You must respect yourself before you would be able to respect money. Anything you do not respect will never be able to stay with you. Respect is equality and that is a reality; what you do not consider your equal will be the catalyst to your downfall. There are laws that govern our existence; that definitely warrants our persistence as whatever you do not respect could potentially destroy you. Like how the law of gravity keeps us grounded on this earth. Our karma keeps us counted so we don't end up dumbfounded; so the concept of one having to pay for another shortcoming does not materialize. So what goes around always comes around and what has not met you yet has not passed you yet.

So the notion of something getting as good as it gets does not apply. Movement requires a circular motion without it everything stands still.

The circular shape is the most important in the universe; let us explore. Mister solar the sun has a circular shape; the moon has a circular shape. The stars have a circular shape; I am suspecting it has something to do with aerodynamics; as movement is common among them none of these remains stagnant or dormant.

Air moves in a circle motion, tornado have that same motion' hot air rises in a circular motion. Waves in the ocean have that same circular motion; tsunamis rise and attack in a circular motion. A shark attacks in a circular motion, a wolf attacks in the same way.

When water drops into water it forms into a circular shape; if you drop anything into stagnant water' it also forms a circular shape.

There is something more significant about that circular shape and I know I have only touched the surface. Attack and destruction comes in a circular form. I am thinking illusion is related to that form.

Bits and pieces are coming together I am hoping that I can put them together and make sense realistically. Illusion is never used in defense, as it is only needed in Au fence; to defeat and destroy as you confuse the core.

As it is never straight up it hides in the crevices, like snakes need grass to hide in to do there laughing and deceiving.

Deceit is a catalyst of defeat; and it got the mind roped in as part of its following, the mind is in a lot of things and it takes good hints' as long as you stress on something the mind is ready to run with it. Anybody at any time could hit there spot if confidence is around; as confidence is a fear buster and it guards you from being underpowered.

Needless to say our mind has affiliations with confidence' as if you could think in your mind that you can do it then you can.

Sometimes stuff comes into your head and they could make you feel Cred. You know your mind is at fault because it is responsible for everything in your head; luckily it could be tweaked that in it is so neat.

The lord implore us to try and our mind wants us to just try and it will take us all the way; why is a try so important because it is the bridge to any accomplishment we all need it to grow so we could show.

I like what I like don't matter what anybody says to me. My mind chooses what I like because it knows what I like' my mind works in my head and it gives me that feeling of confidence. As contemplation takes place before much else could be realized; mind power is once again the catalyst to get things by.

Some lives are controlled by emotion the heart muscle that control life itself. Others are controlled by the head muscle or the brain; these two commodities are responsible for a large percentage of our life decisions. It is being suggested that emotion is more associated with the female specie. But with the advent of the gay community; that theory is strongly being challenge as males are supposedly just as emotional.

And as if it has not been over stated, the mind power also controls our emotions. So how we think and how we act is once again being fueled by our mind. So world domination and in retrospect world destruction is taking its cue from the mind; makes you wonder what doesn't the mind control. From my standpoint anything that matters has the mind to thank.

As the fact of the matter is it is mind over matter literally. The act of love a blind emotion obviously takes its cue from the mind. Although seeing is believing feeling deep feelings is now on par with seeing; How do we feel like that about love, we could do anything just for love; in order to begin understanding the mind, we must be able to understand love. As that is not likely, we are stuck like sap on a tree bark with no contact.

As everything is temporary I am convinced that love is also temporary so harmony is also temporary; the feeling of love is also contrary to many' the ones you are attracted to in the interim does not seem to fit, but love is like a bulldozer an invisible force that seem to persuade you in a certain direction and you cannot hurry or slow it down; so like a bird in a hurricane you just glide in order to survive' so the concept of a soul mate does not bake my cake. As a good woman could be found any day at any time in any country, but one cannot be in many places at the same time; but realistically creed or color does not worth a dollar to the genuine lover, so we are victims of our circumstance' yet another law to keep us dumbfounded.

We exist in moments at a time, each little moment represents a different reality; which will decide when and where we would be happy, one degree off could give us the third degree.

And all this degree stuff plays into that circular narrative, like the rays of the sun one off is a blow off. A little effort could cause you to pivot, when nothing is happening an effort could start something. A little goes a long way it changes your way by staring you another way; choices are good as you never feel like you are backed in a corner' having to deal with the situation of cluster phobia. But a cluster of anything isn't too bad considering' you got strength in numbers not many do alone well. Big and little operates on different ends of the spectrum.

And are intertwined from the bottom up; I feel big every time I try a little, so to belittle me will be futile' haters are advised to just walk on by, advise will be welcomed when asked for' the try is an any day any time kind of high; with no hidden fees it is certainly free to try, experiment on yourself make a commitment with yourself and start loving yourself; if you only begin to trust yourself, others might begin to trust you' in the end of it all it is just about me and you.

Two is a combination that connects in every nation, there is association admiration and fraternization which is easily accomplished between two; but what is needed is for us to find those qualities in ourselves, as the incentive isn't there going through solely activates lonely; but It is part of the process of seeking success' as when you buckle down on the ground you got only you to count on; when things go wrong and they will, when you could count on you that is truly comforting.

We need another for an endorsement imagine if you took that on yourself selfishness could be self absorbing and it also is empowering. Selfishness seems to be an asset these days in light of all this illusion.

You will try in earnest to be if you want to be; we live to achieve so to do that we must produce' a little goes a long way and most times all the way we fluster not' as we are not on the spot a succession of little moves works as well as a big move we don't get over worked, so we won't feel like not working' but before the getting could be had, there must first be the trying, as we all reside in this domination nation that is our portion, sending a message is where the mind game come into the fray.

You could follow someone's act but that won't impact you, satisfaction is only guaranteed if you do you a little' this is me doing me opening up possibilities, I can be someone believable if I believe I am believable' it is currently inconceivable how many more like me don't listen to what is plausible, that inner gut feeling is often unmistakable.

To lead any pact you must make an impact' or you will be limited like someone who is intimidated, as intimidation is an occupation' some lack the for sight to fight day and night, so they aim to convince you that you are not right; there mantra is simply we can't, so you cannot it is self-exorcising and often contradictory.

I am the creator of this realistic tit bit; I describe it as my analogy fusing money and poly; bringing you this concept the commodity of money. I bear no apology being a rookie at this and I call it as I see it, but this money thing is the king on the hill' money is king and queen and we are its subjects, it rules everybody and dominates the [monopoly] its flexibility has the ability to control the fraternity, it is an earthly God and it rules over all other commodities for sure, money controls everybody in the world but a good mind could controls all the money.

So if we can and I know we can keep each others company briefly' this could take more than a yawn, as we take this dive and discover uninterrupted, what has many corrupted, something is secluded and it needs releasing, my inner taught is ready to come out, lets push this out, you know what I am talking about.

My first book giving me my first look from the outside looking into this writing abyss' which contains obvious pitfalls but one cannot be scared of falling as the getting up is when the wondering stops, so that daunting phrase.

If I knew I had it within me, I would of tried before now' but there is nothing like the urgency of now; the time had to be now, it is sometimes scary to try I am in it for the nourishment and not for the accomplishment' so I am already a winner that is my spinner; this is going to deviate all over hay. I got heightened interest and I want in on this, but I do not want a free be, so as I let loose of this juice I am on the job' game on so let us get it on.

Let us experience the plays that would define us in specific ways; as the winner should be the thinker from the get go' but only if we implore the mind. I have tunnel vision that is all I can muster at this point in time and the trier in me is telling me go easy and keeps it steady. Money poly is the world's monopoly, it is not a folly, this combination is joined at the hip and it is a hit, poly or plastic is reaping havoc in many lives welcome to the credit card revolution and as if that was not enough body parts are now a stable and it is not a fable, for female enhancement it has an endorsement. Plastic surgery is now as common as any human. With percentages rising we could have plastic humans as a stable, (really) if not already.

Money and poly is now a lethal combination controlling all the action; light weight and accessible the ultimate tease if you pleased that brings us to our knees, money is master and we are the servants have you ever heard of a servant dictating to their master.

I could go ballistic with this and introduce my temper to this, but I know my temper is the one thing, I cannot get rid of by losing it, so I am going to cool it, to freeze it. Money-poly has manipulation down pack to a science, it is the world's best even without a test because of daily consequences; we are haunted just for not having money. As everything else calls for it we are chasing after money for life and some have the audacity to say it is not about money, when we think we are reeling it in; it is slowly reeling us in, money is the one thing that is capable of changing anybody' that is why everybody is captivated by money.

Our wants have overtaken our needs, no need to deny; it is a worldwide cry as what we want is more bullish, as I see it this seems like mind manipulation to me' although our mind is about domination, it is clear it could be dominated' so our need has conceded and what we want now rules with an iron fist' so our needs are now bog down or mired. So many of us are confused about life in general with questions like why this and why that, when stuff does not make sense. To begin with; it is often suggested that important decision making should be done not with the heart or the emotion, but with the head or brain; although the head is on top; they are both govern by the same power the mind.

What does that say is it important, does it matter what is the fact of the matter; if one read between the lines, what will one find. Will it be enough to draw the line and to fall in line or just ignore the line all together one thing is for sure the mind cannot be ignored.

As the lord cannot be found without exploring the confines of the mind; concentration and contemplation are basic attributes of the mind, which never changes as the basic fundamental principles never changes. One of our goals in life is to have peace of mind; so we can think and worship and accomplish and not be selfish.

These are basic building blocks for betterment and making a genuine statement, for things to at least appear to make sense.

We all want to be good and to do good; but good and good is no good from a human perspective' only the lord is all good and only he can extricate good. As positive needs negative in order to generate power; what is the concept of solar power the source of light in general as we continue to be in the dark. There is so much we do not even know I often wonder why we even bother to get cocky. Only our lord knows why all positive energy gives you positivity. With a ten percent brain utilization on average; our mind continuously bacon's us to try more in order to be more sure and thus accomplish more. As speculation continues to cloud our vision creating endless delusion; as confusion is the cornerstone of illusion. Forgetfulness is brain related so it is mind related as the mind governs the brain; there is some good in all of us and there is some bad in all of us. A battery generates its power that way and we generate our power that way that is the laws under which we are govern.

There is no law that governs the lord and he alone is the law. Just as the mind is not limited to the confines of the brain; the lord is not limited to the confines of the earth' like natural levitation seems unnatural and walking on water invokes so much wonder. There is a spin on everything that is how the brain keeps us in cirque; the spinner leaves you when you lease expect, money leaves you when you lease expect; a joke comes at you until the punch line' then it leaves you. Nothing else seems to be straight up, no wonder the world is corrupt.

To get ahead you need an edge' sometimes it might mean driving a wedge. To rule or conquer one need to divide; as every will not be on the same page at the same time. A strategy is just a policy pass, a curve or a spinner in the ringer. To keeps you in the game' the goal is to make it linger, like when you put a ring on a girl's finger, you just want the love to lingual. A real smile and a fake smile looks the same from the outset; the one that lingers is the real deal' when it doesn't it is no deal.

The look away test works best on the flesh it takes one second to pass the test. Look away then immediately look back' if the facial expression changes in a flash you know you don't want that. As illusion is confusion the smallest is the biggest; how you handle the smallest of things is the way you will handle the biggest. So money and mind is actually intertwined; we disrespect pennies all the time and pretend to respect money all the time' but what we do in spurts little spurts is always what works; so our baby steps are just magnified to become our larger steps, so if you cannot execute little money' you cannot do it with big money, you cannot manipulate a little role what makes you think you could rock a big role.

We teach our self how to handle our self, like we teach others what we like ourselves. More than many love the player, as many more loves to play' the game is loved by the gamer until they stop being a winner. It doesn't matter who or what you are playing if you are not winning you will not feel like playing. As soon as something becomes painstaking you will consider escaping. Medicine is prescribed for pain' otherwise it will be not worth taking. We seek comfort so we must put in an effort, that is why we work so much' we sometimes work too much, smart work is better than hard work' some might think they have a monopoly on smart work. Higher accumulated education does not always translate to higher achievement, as work ethic is a real critic. Achievement is measured at the end of your game, during the game accolades boost the ego and it gets you on the go; so you stand a better chance to show, but all this achieving and performing is of the mind doing. Accelerating the booster in any game, changes the perspective in any game' it is like cruise control that is when you have total control' to some it is mind boggling to others it is captivating; that is the domain of the mind, that helps us to keep achieving' it is not deceiving although sometimes concealing; that is why it is incumbent upon us to do some venturing. So much is hidden as we parade in this illusionary prison.

Doing the time is a prelude to utilizing the time and becoming refined that is connected to unrealized achievements and unheard of performances. Like a diamond hidden in the rough for all its life, not ever glittering. Mesmerizing will be none existent' but as long as one finds themselves' that is hope in itself and ones existence should mean something because we all want to know we existed and contributed, even in this the mind is doing its thing. A sad day is when you don't know what is within you, without a try you are living a lie at some point you need make a point or what is the point. Circumstances produce obstacles before you; to deviate is a good take that is why one needs to be able to make mistakes in life' just as much is realized either way as the difference is so miniscule, if you are going to drive with your hand broke on you will never be able to accelerate; if you are going to venture into anything you cannot be tentative or it will not be positive, the mind game is at work here again if you are going forward it does not help if you are looking backward this is just self explanatory isn't that like taking candy from a baby, because a baby will not be able to stop me. I know of no one who goes in pursuit of mistakes; but unavoidably they occur to teach us you know' but appreciation never comes on the front end, only on the back after the fact when things are already in tack; mistakes gives you contact to unforeseen situations that could be incorporated if realized. It seems to me one learns more from a mistake; but it is never encouraged, why is it always discouraged I guess it is a taste that could be acquired once a trier is hired; but it certainly needs a fearless opponent as natural fear is a deterrent. Some are fearful of trying and some are afraid to try as the unknown is not only home grown it is full grown and it never intends to leave us alone. My present journey is my destination because my destination is my journey as I realize and indorse these insignificant moments piling up, mole hill upon mole hill to become mountainous which is cinnamon's with enormous. Simplicity from where I sit keeps me worked up a little bit; sometimes I wonder and ponder when I do not get it like that. But patience is not my trait, unabated is my wait to make a difference at any moment' as weight in itself is a heavy load. A mind is squandered when it is wasted and a moment is wasted when it is squandered, an opportunity let go is a no go as it has nowhere to go.

I started off this journey on a haunch, then that haunch turned into a bunch, then that bunch turned into bunches of hunches. I could not stop this so I had to drop this while it was hot to make it count. It is like this and it was like that, the big fix to anything, nothing is out of reach because money is the big reach, money could reach anything, its flexible stretchable and bond-able, nothing is more useable and feasible, so it is reasonable to call it practicable by applying the brain you are introducing the mind to the game as the brain is physical and the mind is always mental. I must admit though I am wrapped up like a mummy because of money I said never me now it is playing me at will, still I have a glimmer of hope as I know at the end of the day it takes my vole-entering for anything to work.

I find myself getting hooked to money because of the power of money, could one have power without having money from my perspective silly I think not, but that is just my view how about you It could be reviewed and one could arrive at a different result, as conditions changes every day, every time there is a situation change a game is change. It is all in the game, money could be a friend when you have it and an enemy when you do not. As money gives your ideas by telling you this and telling that, then you begin to get the feeling that you could do just that, confidence grows and confidence shows to let someone show, because money is the show and it is not only for show. But it always lets you know that you can change any show as dictation steps in, money matters as money is the matter but of course mind is always over matter and that is the fact of the matter. Out of reach is a breach anything that is out of our reach is resented like a leach' but money brings everything within reach When something goes over your head it makes you wonder' or to incorporate another analogy like the concept of the wind, where did it come from and where does it go to. I guess that is the definition of a conundrum. It is realistic and hypnotic, the magic of money is every bodies business, anybody who is anybody, depends on this commodity for mobility and stability' as long you are not referring to or including spirituality, money is all and it could help you to not fall.

Money is the wheel of prosperity, it could turn anyone easily' although illusion plays a part for the most part. Everyone have their price, that could make everything turn out nice, it gives us humans that feeling of accomplishment, it is what we strive for as we live, it is the only thing that gives like Jesus, that's why it is now rival-ling Jesus. Money could keep us achieving, as we aspire and perspire. It gives us a little independence although temporary, it eliminates total dependence. This all came about, as I made a turn on the money roundabout.

Venturing into business could be a risky business, there is constant growing pains when trying to grow your business, one thing is present and always current, you need a live wire to distribute the current, in order to keep anything alive you need the current, what is that current, money is that current, it runs the world, that currency has a monopoly. I call it money poly as it pulls you anywhere it wants to.

So it now has worldwide domination, without it all we will be or could be, is a mythical maybe because we would not even place in the race, standing out would be a myth, like pleading the fifth it could still inflict and create a conflict' you will be present but everyone will think you are absent, you will not stand out, nothing that you do will ever count, everyone will push you over, to be a push over is unacceptable and unfavorable. I am not teacher/d up, just fired up; I do not have a degree, just pedigree.

I go with my instinct as I try things to find out things, in this innovation age I have come of age as I occupy my inner stage. I try at every opportunity that is my simple policy. As we know an innovator is a trier, the simple term was just replaced by one that was more sophisticated; innovator is like having the answer leaving no room for error as the answer is the solution. Only when you try out could you find out, so when you try new things you find out new things, so experience is now playing second fiddle to the trier, although experience is the best teacher, the innovator becomes the principal.

Doing things the old way, has given way to new ways of doing the old things, well, more choices are more voices, with more focused eyes, you are more likely to hit the bulls-eye of the mind which is called real power.

The steam and the esteem, is only achieved when money is on the scene, it seems it is a universal language as you could imagine, you could call it bilingualism and quote it verbatim, the effect is the same' money is the stuff of which everything is made.

While masquerading as a ghost writer I discovered I could be a host writer, that discovery made me feel my inner strength; like a muscle man with a dumbbell.

With some tweaking and believing in myself, the charade or now lost its appeal' seeing that this is my coming out parade and I am trying to get made.

I am making my claim because I think I got game, so I am better off keeping it simple, I have discarded my ghost armor and replaced it with my host armor, as I am contemplating catching the writing fire' it comes so natural I swear I studied it for my thesis, believe it. I write as a hobbyist, I am not trying to convince like a lobbyist.

I am just a purist seeking the clearest path to comprehending substancive. But to be a specialist, you must insist and cease to desist; I must go at it as I am feeling it. This bug has bitten me and that has smitten me, now I am thinking maybe there is a place for me or I am being confused by that bubbly feeling inside, as it is customary, you always want to share your bubbly typically' Just to show that you made it as making it is showing it, life is about the show' even if you do not show, you want someone to know that you did something; and you are not about nothing, as nothing from nothing leaves nothing' being a physical deficiency that blows up the ego, control as you steadily grow.

I got something for you to chew on; it might go on, so sip some water and let us get it on. Those who have it say it is not about the money, but when you do not have any you know it is only about the money, it always is about the money like breathing, you cannot live without breathing and you cannot live without money.

The commodity of dominance giving credence to domination as a reference, everyone from everywhere seeks some of this commodity.

Money and more money, it is all about money, it is only about money, if you do not have any, you better get busy, as whatever we are fortunate to be doing' it is for money surely. Money is domination and persuasion, it has always been that bate on a line to pull you in line; it works well so I guess all is well, as it satisfies anyone with a vivid imagination.

Money has that persuasion factor, some call it that it factor and it always satisfying.

I look around in amazement and wonder why we do not capitalize on endorsing ourselves because if we could push ourselves we do not need much else as when we become self-motivators we flex the powers of terminators.

I guess it comes down to confidence, only when confronted could it be compounded, we need to challenge ourselves down to a science, it is that important and only then could we become important. You go by your gut feeling which is an interesting feeling, it helps you to pursue, which presents an issue, laying the groundwork for discovery.

When it comes to oneself, the discovery is the recovery because the assembly is complete, just the plug in is needed and we are ready to analyze and tantalize. Acknowledging your self is the heart of the matter, why does it matter because everyone matters as everyone does it differently, that blend is needed to the end as each one has a mind of there own can you imagine two minds working together with the same goal.

Realistically nothing else matters more than yourself, if we believe we will achieve' that is plausible when we believe in our self as minor or when we believe in the lord as major.

Although it is an imaginary line to rope you in, at some point, everybody got to fall in or you will be falling out. Picture yourself free falling and flipping into thin air that is enough to get you thinking, of your mortality right there, as in the end we just need to blend' as we acknowledge the end because when it is over it is over, there's no room for a makeover' so be satisfied while you alive, so you will be satisfied on your last ride.

Everything crumbles without money like a house of cards it works as a stabilizer, only when you place your full stop, will it drop you off' it has all of us dangling from our coat tails, there is always a need to play another game' because the potential exists more money to do this and that. It is the world best prop to keep you up, while you try to climb to the top you probably will not be in whatever you are doing without that money prospectus. We do it all for the money, so adapting is preparing in the interim. Money is debatable and that is something notable, its presence always enhances any present, the feeling inside tantalizes and there is no feeling of compromising Money is a world regulator and the most popular negotiator.

Not too difficult to decipher, its flexibility has the ability to convince. Money is selfish so we become like it and it is customary and capable of juggling any memory, it is clear we now worship that commodity called money. Although it might be done inadvertently the idea of money is lovely.

Because of its gift of achievement although temporary, money isn't designed to be a disappointment. It levels any playing field and it is the art of the deal. As when you have it no need to scream' because it speaks for you as it works for you silence in its presence is golden, why warp. It is the only commodity that is capable of replacing a human presence, as in their absence the void is filled like a windmill on a hill, the cooling effect does the rest.

But the way we chase after it relentlessly' our disappointment is certain searching and not ever finding, the cost of living creates a tough living we become disappointed in our selves when things do not pan out. Money takes away that melon colic feeling, the deal is money is the real deal with the real feel, tangibility gives it that ability to perceive' but sometimes it deceives and makes us sneeze, then we realize we are not in control we just adjust the controls.

What backs you up when the going gets tough, money is that prop to keep you up, a back rest or a treasure chest you name it, the flexibility of money keeps everybody easy. And if by chance you want to be tough, money is the stuff tough is made of. What has the right away, on the straight away every day, money all the way? It is that driver that could take you higher, on any day in different ways because of the flexibility' to win big one must risk big if there is a silent hurt' it could treat you like a jerk, as long as you decide to put in some work then things could work. The acceptable way is playing me oh money, feel free to mislead me, but do not leave. Don't you ever think of leaving me, you are my money. I hope you got me because I got you thinking all about me.

We are anchored at the hip, money you give me that comfortable fit. No creases or blemishes our fixation on money is a typical obsession. A little money makes your life a memorable experience everyone wants to have that experience. Although it is temporary like ones memory, believe you me, the problem is and always will be, we try to convert a temporary situation, into a permanent one. As long as I could remember, money was always a luxury even before I knew the specifics. These days money is like an Epiphany, surpassing even the luxury. I am still waiting for money to endorse me hopefully. With my luck that isn't likely, I don't have the pedigree. My memories linger like my karma it is going to be with me forever. It appears and disappears, you have moved on but some things cannot. Like a moment in time will be frozen in time. Everything has its time and place like your space. Which creates the real justification around your waist that gave you the taste to indulge it in the first place. We are in it for the money, it is what it is, money is what it is. A worldwide exodus is because of one purpose, people are trying to handle the stress of not having what they want out of life by making money their focus. Money is that commodity that is capable of juggling any bodies memory, with that kind of clout, no wonder money could make you pass out. Although I grew up without much I was sure about this much. I didn't want to remain without much. That dream still exists to dismiss it would be Nonsensical, trying to achieve these days is almost Mythical, an imprint made is an imprint saved, this game of life structures your life. It is understandable as you create your revised identity, the old experience might seem to impede your progress a bit. We cannot assimilate our foundation, it is always provided for us by someone other than number one, like you will provide for someone else it is all about bridging the gap and filling the blank spot, that is why you do not need to look back, it will always be on your back. Memories are for life even when things go wrong, only you could turn things around. That is if you think they are worth turning around, the world is a get around' as you go around and move on, a lot of times moving on turns our Tojo on as our pride is engaged Importance is an individual concept, you put importance to what is important to you, it has nothing to do with being well to do or not, that is one of the very few things that we actually have control of in life. It is truly a made up thing, we each carry on somebody else thing, what we think is irrelevant for the most part we serve each other like a servant in most parts. Only as we serve could we be served, it is the law of equilibrium' balance is substance. The chain is as strong as the weakest link some of us think we are independent and not dependent on the average, so we do not have to do the job of salvage. Who you rescue may not be able to rescue you and who helped you may not need help. A helping hand is necessary, if only to promote continuity. The state of being deluded cannot be construed as being visionary, although it glides as it slides in place. In this world unlikely is most likely, a major component that causes real confinement, once you are confused it limits you like a noose around you. Only realization could save you and once you get it you will not ever forget it, to get satisfaction everybody needs somebody, even if they are a no body because everybody is part of somebody. The mantra we are forced to hammer is, get money or everything will past you, earn money or poverty will claim you, without money society do not need you, the reason for that is society wants money from you too. This Monstrosity needs individuals in order to rotate, only endless labor will fit the mole in order to get close to the pole, climbing up though has its own ups and downs. Nothing is permanently stable, that is what creates the fable, you work your way up to a point, then things changes as it wants, welcome to the world of stocks and bonds, you gain a lot and you lose a lot, if you cannot afford to lose what you got, you better stay out stay out of that. The bribe or bate is how we relate as we travel on the interstate, debating is security for ones future we are either doing miles or megabytes in style as it is a free style. It is up to you to take your bite, to a degree we are playing the same game, maybe in a different lane but feeling the same pain. Get money is the mantra, get money it will help you to go far' without that money you become a statue. Getting anywhere will take some money, the whole world is into that concept of money, it is what everyone respects and uses as a tool to deal with stress. But the key is holding on to money, by investing in money, if it is not working for you, it will not be of help to you' therein lies the problem we rather keep it close disallowing it to work, that is why a wall flower never gets any brighter' as it cannot simmer. Money is like the brain, it could help you in sun or rain, you cannot stop that money train but a strategy could ease your pain. You know that a strategy could solve any problem with a clear head there is nothing to dread. As if money knows, there it comes and there it goes only a strategy could make it your own. We are in for blows as we chase money, a good strategist will beat you mercilessly as money does to us daily which is like an optical illusion, it is never where you think it is, and as if we are awake but blindfolded no wonder we seem to be dumbfounded in our daily undertakings. We are sacrificing our entire life to earn money, our spirituality remains a mystery, we are saying lord help me but that help is to get some money. The churches are running the same money game, anyone is really fair game, the manipulative concept is entrenched in the church tent no wonder the church and state was connected, maybe they are still associated.

Every time you tide it disappears like spent time, are we paying for our spiritual ride you think the lord needs money, when he has everything he needs. We need to spend time knowing him, time changes the tide but we don't have the time. We always want more time as we used up our spent time. Spending time in his reverence is the only thing that makes sense the lords business is now a business, if you are in the business of the lord that is certainly your business, drunk or sober one must mind their own business. As we all know every business is to make money, but we sometimes confuse it don't it. Money is now our lord and savior, that's what we worship to accomplish independence, no one likes to be dependent at least money makes you codependent, but you run the risk of having us twisted like a twister, whenever it touches down you know it is disaster. Money is a spectacle to behold in this envious world, get money and your life is easy because it takes care of the formalities. Preoccupation with money sounds like a monopoly and it is playing everybody. Song writing is part of my game, it has helped me to expand and transcend, and diversifying has so far been interesting. I am connecting with the art of wording, which is a necessary for articulating and communicating, with communication comes an assortment of options. No one knows me yet, so I guess I am new and fresh, untested so I am building a backbone to be able to stand predominate, in this finicky world. Writing is surely interesting, I never realized how interesting. Much thinking was going into thinking about things, without putting down a marker, you cannot know if you are an over stepper. If you have not found yourself, how can you be able to identify yourself?

I am making a dash contemplating a splash, as I face reality potentially I feel I am a lyricist equip-end with fitness you are being the witness to this money business, some say it is not about the money, but is has always been about the money. All things take money unless you exist under the grid, there is a reason why the lack of money, could make you teary eyed at will, without it existence will take a lot of persistence. To do this to do that you need money for a fact, what am I going to do without money in my act I will fall flat, of course I will have to pack and head for the back, I would not stand out I will have to stay out. Money has that presence to give you representation, once you got it you in it, so game on, this strangle hold is gone, you and me is evident like the evidence, money is the instrument of consequence, you could only play if you got the instrument, it is dominating and intimidating to say the least, what has been trending could definitely be daunting, the love affair with money and the acquisition of money isn't a folly, I am fixated on money it does not matter in what category.

I have lived without money that did not trill me or interest me one bit, so I made a pledge to not sit on the fence, but to jump in to get in, because nothing is more pivotal, just the commitment felt awesome.

This single commodity has everybody going crazy, you cannot get enough, because it never seems to be enough, it gives you access to the good stuff, this domination is far and wide, it is actually worldwide, money dominates as it Permeates. The domination of money is also a perspective terminator without it you do nothing achieve nothing and experience nothing, economies fall flat without that money act in fact, participation in the action is now a natural Phenomenon that has caught on thanks to the domination of the persuader, it is what it is so let us call it what it is, money is domination, it is elusive and conducive and makes some people massive, but the temporary nature is the deal breaker as we want it forever. This system in which we are tied to as we try to strive is all so true.

The fight is intensive, that is what makes us passive. Realizing without money we are no match, our relevance is irrelevant, becoming nonsense and an incense as getting respect will be stretch. The great domination action is a two headed monster, endless assistance in one instance and reliance in another merciless and ruthless on the reverse of that domination' what an awkward situation to dwell on, but like anything else circling your situation with the capability of termination at the drop of a hat' enough to make you tip your hat. Monopoly personified what a ride and or a slide, a creator and a destroyer all in one. Money does not really need any one, but everybody needs money that's a certainty, to exist on this earthly, money is permitted without it forget it. To be in demand that's when you command, because once you realized what you got in your hand, that simple fact gives you the tact so you act and you could run with that. Availability of the commodity called money could turn a zombie into somebody, who could help or manipulate another, because of the power of money.

The system volunteers that power to anyone with the money, it does not discriminate or incriminate' even if you stole it from a friend in need to satisfy your greed, the money door stills opens up to you' and you flourish for just a bit before you lose it. Money is powerful and it is a bounty that is powerful, once you get some you feel awesome and the power is laid upon you like a crown, so money is power because the power is money, with it you are with it, without it you are not it and not in it You play with an advantage because of money, you could take advantage because of money, you can make the rules because of money, so you can break the rules when you have money. For once the playing field is level, you got it you are promoted to that special status because you got the seed money indeed, how you got it is irrelevant, to money there is a reverence. Manipulation is an occupation remember that, there is a reason why it has become so popular. You could get manipulated at home you could get manipulated at work. You could get manipulated at church I didn't mean to rock that boat. Church goers worldwide have an aversion of the proverbial mark of the beast. I personally have an aversion for not having money, is there a connection may be but let us wait and see the changes comes around the bend just when you think it is the end, a dead end is where things mend, new life follows the old life a new course has no recourse because of survival of course. If you cannot do anything without the mark of the beast, right now you cannot do anything without money, the gravity of this is the reality of this, that mark of the beast must be connected to money. Although waiting is a heavy load it is border line hypothetical when money comes a baggage comes, choose what you want and discard what you don't want the human factor is major, if you bring in minor you on the burner, as it resembles mediocre that is a choker. To describe the language of money to me it is priceless, as long as you do not have it you pay a price. Most times you don't even need a permit to make things perfect to a lot of us success is major excess. Abundance without consequence of course, that is the rich person's discourse, they could flex their muscle with authority being in familiar territory that is why not having money is a worry to everybody, some of us is not that lucky. We all know that and not having money have a consequence in itself to others success is a permanent recess when you can afford to have a permanent recess that might be considered success there you go. But money talks and even barks, the elite have it down packed to a scienceWe are wrapped up in there fortune which is our misfortune.

In this system of manipulation, you need your own fortune because the system has its hand out looking for a payout. When that money machine goes to work the ordinary starts to choke there is so much work you cannot afford to not work. Here is the kicker as we are relegated you earn just enough to eat sleep and pay the rent, the money do not make a dent for bills payment' some are always deferred although not preferred but continuity must be preserved. So you back to work trying to make it work, another joke in your chest of jokes. But when you work hard you learn hard and you become hard remembering the lessons you had.

God must be a work man to come up with the human that is why our actions give us satisfaction, as what we do define us and identifies us thus authenticating us forever. Any specie that could learn anything and adapt to anything that's convincing, no wonder dominion was given to the human to ignite interaction in every nation. If only we could unite, there will be no reason to fight then energy could be used to energize and not disenfranchise the masses. I guess it depends on if your interest is helping of hurting the broke. To the upper tee, being broke is a joke so you are treated like a joke, that really hurts and isn't a joke. For something to be laughed at or jeered at being on the lower end of the spectrum is something you learn to get accustom to and tolerate The unfortunate plight of the poor who will forever be needing more. Trying to change your cycle you straddle on the work peddle. Your muscle will hold out for so long till cramps come on, keeping up is good as gone but you know you cannot give up your back is against the wall. You could get squished and scraped off the wall, you could fall and be trampled in front of the wall, or you could push back using the wall that is a fact.

Attack or you will be attacked that positively destroys the negative but it's a dream it seems, as soon as things begin to work. Minor disagreements create arguments, the money is now a tool to be used to rule and break the rule.

Unrest is suspect to make us all fail the test, humans destroying humans trying to dominate like the money can. To dream is believable only humans make the dream unbelievable. It is us against us what is the fuss we all have to leave like Jesus. I am wrapped up mummified by money, sometimes I even get terrified by money, seeing what it could do and undo. That money it's beyond me one reason civilization has been continuous the power of money as a consequence. The pain and the gain over and over again is insane, do I need to clarify then why explaining has been varying. Is it not about the money, it has always been the money, although money is necessary, less money is less enemies but if you think the money is the enemy, you better think again carefully. Friendlies are a dime a dozen and enemies are a dime a dozen, the only difference is they are intertwined and refined, one could replace the other like flipping on a dime. Once the situation fits it does not have to be forced, a friend could front as an enemy and an enemy could front as a friend, as long as you comprehend that, you will be in control to the end. Once you know that nothing could happen that you would be surprised of. Being misled would be unheard of, illusion will be temporarily harness. So the enslavement on earth would have a relaxed grip. Somebody have to do some work, that's all we got to do here on earth anyway is work. Our best examples and samples are about work trying anything is actually a joke Repeating anything is definitely work, it is work to perceive and ultimately achieve, the process is worthless but maybe not useless. Good things sometimes come in minute packages. The design outside could mislead about the inside.

Around the corner most definitely is going to be a surprise. The buildup never chalks up to the hype or type. Excitement is overrated, it only makes things complicated. An individual persons head could be dead to excitement.

So anything would suffice, neutrality is always a distinct possibility that is why silence is golden. Private autonomy is a specialty like a bluff, only you actually know if and when you had enough. But how much is enough, is it when you say enough.

But it varies like pastries the mystery is the mastery.

Preparation is the occasion to marvel and fiddle diddle time is multiple.

The wisdom of being ready will always keep you steady.

What is up with money and me I already know the deal the chances of it liking me is a maybe I am just a no body needing money like everybody. There are bigger and better priorities to enhance these activities. Out talk sight is outta mind I haven't been around for much time. I am paying my dues maybe I could get amused. I know I belong because I am trying strong you cannot go wrong if you want to be a winner, a winger is destined to be a winner. They are mobile and ready for hire decision time is all the time so does not keep you confine for a long time. It comes and goes everyone knows, where it goes to god knows, because I lack money poor me I should not be left out or feel left out. My importance is still authentic I am still capable of contributing to the final outcome money or not I am giving it all, I think that should be close enough at the end of the day that is to say who goes or stay. Knowing money call the shots anyway who got it does just that. The domination has dominion over all, if you think you are powerful without money, you not at all. Money is a brace around your waist helping you to keep straight and hold the pace, out of step is out of line and out of line is out of mind. Every time my outlook is my in look, that's what I see when I look in most of us are just front in. There is obviously something not working, revealing is informing and conforming to the deal, but I perfectly well understand. You try to handle a situation the best you can, off course dealing with human takes tact for a fact you never know what to expect. Like a corner view invisible to everyone, only when you turn the corner, does everything become clearer and visible, so it is simple like squeezing a pimple. Around the corner is uncertain, that's when everybody starts guessing. Unknowing could be annoying and uninteresting, it might be helpful not fretting, It does not do any helping. If you not in control of a situation that is life control comes and goes in every life time comes and goes. As we also know there is one major guarantee, nothing remains the same forever unless it was provided by the power of powers. The sun the moon and the stars never change but that's another level in this uncertain game.

Mother earth and father water alternate with each other, layers cover over and create a new starter, major and minor always work together humans and animals were always part of the equation. Possible interaction likely but considered hardly that does not make it unlikely. It is funny how I am being driven at this point in time.

Us humans got dominion because of the brain power and money now have dominion over us because its power to accumulate stuff.

Some of which we could do without half the time. But what do I know, is being civilized storing up treasures in vain, then we are causing ourselves pain, why would someone cause themselves pain when they have a brain, don't ask me why I only made an observation. You could come to your own conclusion. I am not schooled up in that stuff, but something seems rough to me that's just me' silly me. Or am I being schooled by my own taught.

I don't have any resort but to report my findings keeping it fenced up make me stressed up so I had to bring it up. Let us be better yet, let me be realistic for a fix up minute, I know myself. I am falling victim to the domination, I know I made a pledge long ago to seek money and don't let go.

Before you go like, is that so, for me it happened ages ago, when I had zero. I really taught it was going to be temporary, now it is a permanent seek, but I cannot relent. I made an appointment with making it, at lease it beats faking it. My investment is in me, I have sampled scraping through between me and you no can do, I want to drive through so the commodity domination is the bridge on which I pass over, so it is not my enemy. I am currently busy because of one commodity, that same commodity have me breathing easy supplying my needs when needed. When it is not around I tend to frown as if everything has gone so wrong as long as money is around, I am happy like a clown.

I am not being a brute, I am just telling the truth, money could change me as it could anybody, only God do not need anything. Money does not need anybody so it abuses everybody.

But every human needs money that is why we are vulnerable. Maybe but if we have less needs we would need less, but it is impossible to tell someone with nothing that they need nothing and it is impossible to tell someone with everything that they don't need something else.

They would think you are full of yourself and something just hit me. Is money more important to the rich or the poor is anybody sure' each one could answer for sure. Furthermore would the rich benefit more are you sure, the poor have needs but the rich are needy to, whose needs are more critical in this virtual universal' to each there own.

I beg to differ; justification is based on what indication. Is it on a pee-tee party or on one of those wealthy parties, at the end of the day' what could you say. Is it observation, to be given authentication. Is it longing or craving or maybe plain old wanting.

The squeaky wheel gets the grease because attention was brought to it, what about suffering in silence is that important or unimportant, acknowledgment could be given to the known, what about the unknown' the lord has done so much for me half of what is unknown to me I hope he never forgets me. The elite have it wrapped up like a mummy and I continue to feel worry. I lack money and everything takes money, living and also dying relates to money. My disappointment of me having less money has given me an appointment with acknowledgment and endorsement. Being a have not does not mean I should or would have not. Frugality with money definitely helps you and me to face reality. You should not spend what you didn't earn that is something you just have to learn, adjustments makes statement to keep you in agreement.

No pain is no gain and time spent is time went. Preparation is the law of that I am sure, when you are prepared you have no fear even if fear is there your taught will be elsewhere.

Like on the dream, you need a dream because, without a dream it is easy to sweep you off your feet. Beginning any dream could be risky like false history. But you stay the course of course, you have no recourse, to understand the course, you need to ride the horse. Anyone could cry good try, but you will only get teary eyed, you need to be wide open eye, if your try is going to be worthwhile.

Obstacles hit like a brick, so your skull got to be thick, you must be prepare to take a licking. So if it comes you are prepared for the coming. But when it comes to the lord, not many are prepared for the coming' as everyone is scared of dying. Take a hit and fake a hit, bluffing is good for something, sometimes you have to call your bluff you are now equal when it becomes a ritual, practice falling so when you fall it will not phase you at all. It is time to get it on, courage under fire averts disaster. Pretense has consequences, remember to not settle yourself and get too comfortable. In case your nemesis should step up, the reason will be to take you out. If prepared you will not lose your head and become sightless. We learn when we are right and we learn when we are wrong. Through it all we learn more when we go wrong, but we are fixated on being right, as we are taught to be right, in the light of being right, I guess that is all right. Reality dictates and never hesitates, truth is a realistic pill. You cannot fool yourself even if you try, would you try just to satisfy a hunch, you cannot hide from yourself, even if you close your eyes and cannot see yourself, you would still be conscious of your living self.

Because you learn as you go the learning comes as you go. If you get stagnant or dormant you become absent life lessons are real lessons sometimes you gr-eave sometimes you feel as if you get touched though, you on your way to go, that touch is like major it is a door opener to the inner stuff.

When a sinner get to experience that outer stuff, we think that is enough.

Realization knows that you know, and you could explain to someone why it is so, it's a belief structure driven by confidence which has a major consequence. Self- realization precedes god realization only when you have found yourself could you find your god self. If you don't know what you are capable of would you believe what God is capable of.

God implores us to do one thing above each and everything, it is not only humans but animals too, just try it is why we live, just try you could even be still, it will be good for you when you try, when we learn how that's how we get to know how, not trying will limit your know how. You cannot accelerate if you are tipping the brake, as we run the race. This marathon called life will change what happen in our lives, places will change and faces will change at different stages.

Even our lead will change, so we got to give and take, it's a game of high stakes each one must teach one, that goes for everyone, some think they are better, realization begs to differ. There is never an identical scenario, so who is to know what they don't know, after the fact is good but before the fact is always better. Help at random and work in tandem there is never a good time to do anything or to try anything but don't do nothing, just try something. Good things await the trier; they are always in the running to be hired. The name has changed but the game continues to be the same, it's now innovator a new outlook on an old in look.

The trier is the author of such a book I am connected hook line and sinker. With money being the dinker, without the money it will be a sinker. I will have no power, we will have no power, money is the driver I am just the rider, the mirror image goes with the image, the reflection is void of intention I am not even certain to be a survivor, with every decision to be made money will be the final save, if there are restraint or constraints, money saves the day. If I concoct a cool idea, only money could take it further, so if I don't have a little something nothing doing, that's demoralizing.

To bridge and full any gap for a fact, money is the thing to do that. The money act is the leader of the pact, it is never cumbersome that is awesome. Something like that will invigorate any situation.

Its flexibility is acceptable that's no trouble; with that kind of status no wonder it is a major focus, when money is present that in itself is a present. When money disappears or is dormant that happens in a flash, that dominant machine brings everything to its knees like a cold freeze. Money is the save and it treats us all like its slave, some of us cave, as we try to pave our way each and every day, the fight is in the bight. You could chew the contents of your bite, chew it right and you win the fight. We learn gradually and we earn gradually, we breathe gradually and we achieve gradually, so belief should come gradually because relief is going to come gradually.

Like realization belief gives you a huge relief, positive is never destructive and it is your prerogative, weather you want to be attentive or even sensitive, it is informative though and always helpful when you know. Money is time and time is money, if you have time you could have money because it takes time to make money that makes everybody uneasy. That's why some fall for the quick fix, a quick entrance and a quick exit like the bee syndrome pollinating quick. It is understandable wanting without much trouble, but you get out what you put in, that's old school the original rule sacrifice, not nice if you in for the heist, a taker will just take with a straight face and take again and again.

A giver will always give if they have to give, in our system today you take what you get and what you get you are being trained to be selfish and even ruthless. Some will take all that you have and keep all that they have and wouldn't even budge or give it a second taught. I guess ones conscience is flexible and manageable.

Turning a blind eye is becoming easy to come by, with practice anything could become perfect Some kids don't share I wonder if their parents did, some adults don't share I guess it isn't rear, so what if I care. The journey is the destination and the destination is the journey, when you get there who cares, reaching there was more than hot air, we remember moments that's potent, giving us confidence. A good influence is like a good consequence, all is good that is good. Mountains are made from mole hills, so you could conquer a mole hill before a mountain. Small steps are designed to be positive to remove the doubts created by negative taught.

Baby steps seems to be perfect steps, as we get older we want to widen our steps. But our try steps are still baby steps anything you start in life takes baby steps, anything you think in life take baby steps, anything you dream in life is a baby step. The start-up of anything is a baby step that is why a child could lead us realistically, experience is a good teacher but innovation is the principal the principle is thinking outside the box, bringing new ways to do old stuff. That will keep you out of the box and that in itself is a plus.

Confinement isn't refinement it could create an assortment like procurement, the principle of simplicity is easy. Among the complicated it is relegated although tolerated, its mystified as you read through the lines and the money comes with conditions like love and seduction. Money could make a common breed a special breed. Superficial as it may seem to be, we could agree to disagree, money changes your lane and your game it does not matter what you into or if you are well to do, things come to you. I guess money brings them to you. When you have money you could afford to live and afford to die. Obstacles are just particles, the rich go by like a fly, money could make you and also break you, and it could dominate you and incriminate you, as you try to make a better you. Maybe a more comfortable you is always a realistic possibility if you persevere naturally. Faces and places will change around you, some will be left behind most likely will take it unkind, as you explore your upward climb every time. You are dammed if you do and you are dammed if you don't.

If you won't you on your own, dealing with the unknown is well known you are not expected to be known, a no show will be expected but if you show up then you did not flop. If you don't respect money you are living a folly, so you will always be melon coley, not the place to be, there is always more than what meets the eye, sometimes you don't see what is right in your eyes. Only realization could enlighten you, like your animal instinct, it hits you like magic, then you feel like magic' realizing somethings we might think are unrealistic ends up being so real' by having a real feel. Money makes the rules and also the news, when you don't have money you abide by the rules. The system dictates, get money or you are going contrary, get money to make life easy because the system wants it's bit from your little bit.

Don't you ever forget it if you don't have anything to give the system does not care if you live You must have to rule so a have not cannot rule to call a shot you must have a shot, if you don't that was your shot. A ruler is a controller drunk or sober the owner of the dollar always gives the order. This side is mine that side is thine as long as you don't cross over things will be fine. I could do yours but you cannot do mines a sucker gets played continuously like monopoly. One see what they want to see being oblivious could or could not be obvious what is on your plate usually determines how you play. I am dumfounded by what money can do it is real as can be to me. To use a chess analogy for clarification and simplification, I am the rook or even the pawn in the game enduring pain again and again. Money is king and queen if you know what I mean providing meals and making dreams a reality. It seems money is synonym with mobility, no money is just a travesty and disability, sometimes I think money avoids me like the plague. Incarcerated in a cage at every stage, to have it I must go get it so to count on it I have to key it in. Unlocked I have no luck; I could count on it only if it is locked in, then it does the trick and gives me my fix. There is no substitute to the money kit, it does tricks and it even has wings. It will fly away if it is not locked away, you cannot trust it to stay anyway. It is attracted to more money like birds of a feather it flocks together. Money could be a pleasure although a temporary pleasure, realistic and sadistic are other ways to describe it. Some go ballistic over it I guess it is what it is one major thought it is a legitimate monopoly that isn't a folly. To get ahead you need it, if you don't have it forget it, having it keeps you alive with pride and rejuvenated inside, it has the power to enhance your natural smile and it is healthy to have some. With some you will be welcome, it will always be your guide, if it is staying away continuously, it is no mystery your game needs a little tweaking, to convince it about staying. If there is more to be made it will be in the game over and over again it gets lonesome being the only some, knowing that has the potential to be awesome. Money works best in an investment setting test, keeping it close to your chest is actually best Being considered good and bad it keeps you on your toes, juggling could be troubling when you don't know what you are wanting. If you learn your craft at least in part, before you start then the try will be worth it when you have something to show for it. Everything is temporary like your money and your memory. Cherish it while you have it because one day you might not have it, use it like you could lose it, one day you might not have it. There have been many with plenty and currently they don't have any. Some even won the lottery few years later they falter, but poverty accepts anybody like anybody accepts a token it is only supposed to be temporary, it is a launching pad as you tinker with your game plan. Roll over and do your make over, because it isn't over till it is over a smile is a frown turned upside down. Money could keep that smile year round. Nobody is giving away money so we must find a way to make money stay. It is up to yourself to motivate yourself; bluff yourself to sight yourself keep this quiet, you don't have to cause a riot. Repeat it enough till your belief comes, it is tough work your belief is your relief. If you believe the same you could achieve the same, silence is golden while you wobble in trouble excitement in silence is a personal endorsement. I can do it do it I know I can do it, if you repeat it repeat it repeat it in time you will believe it because we believe what we hare that's crystal clear. Sometimes it is unfair the truth is not always what we here but we believe it I swear. A bate gives access to the taste why not give your own self a taste, because a taste is a taste, make haste and don't let it waste. The mind is awesome like that, you could tinker with stuff just like that you lead it will follow, it could be sometimes shallow. Time is older than respect and honor, so time should always be honored, if you have time you are alive, if you out of time by bye. We say enough is enough but we can never get enough, while some are expanding others are contracting. It goes without saying, take a chance on something, take a chance on someone make yourself that someone. If you do not take a chance you will lose your chance, you are your only chance to enhance your existence Reach out and try out or later you may be crying out because time is out. The limit is basically nothing more will fit no room to move even if you disapprove you cannot improve. I guess society created that proverbial box or idiom which is now a go to phrase. It is society way of labeling me as it contemplates on me. Fox holing me is trying to control me, but like air confining me to my little space will not limit me to handle me. The floods gates are washed away per say, I am sailing away on my terms and in my way, raft riding first class. To differentiate me from other starts, I cannot be taken apart. I was never made up, because I showed up here does not mean I am stuck here. What brings could carry, money brings so it would carry harmony to families worldwide. But there is a kicker here is where things differ, financial bliss is not a myth. But to continuously expect it is a myth. When the system manipulates because it deviates from the norm adjustments changes Everything in the game never stays the same, on the other hand manipulation demands what it can when it can, what you earn is not yours alone there is a hand out turning your pockets inside out. That's the fall out, life is fragile you must be agile, when there is no money it helps no body, anything you want to do will be futile. You feel like a rejected feline, there is no spring in your steps, your face is now visibly upset, out of sight is out of mind, and it is like that most times. Easy becomes difficult when visibility is called into account. You do not respect what you do not see, that is why the concept of lord is a may be, with endless possibilities that just confuses it for us. We are hoping for a place in heaven but cannot imagine dying. Obsess with the body, our earthly spectacle which is a temporary receptacle, that is just recyclable, blinding us and deceiving us, because some of us think we are the focus, their isn't nothing more ludicrous. There goes the mind again going along with the deceiving game; simple belief is temporary until realization arrive putting doubts into oblivion. Fiction is a depiction of some ones imagination, is not dreaming someone imagination, or did I come to the wrong conclusion, I guess it is my imagination, it is an action never the less. You might think it is far fetch, it is close like a finger from another finger Everything is connected So any action could cause a chain reaction As I see it money is cede and it is never free, it is only about money it has always been about money it will always be about money anyone who say it is not about money already have money. It is so reel to me now it is clear as natural air. This domination have spiritual proportions, although we have to leave it all here, the churches insist it will help to get you up there somewhere, it is kind of unfair. Money is the target like the Scottish loving haggish, even the preacher is on the money run, the teacher is on the money run, of course the lawyer is on the money run and it goes on and on. No wonder why we delicate our entire working life towards earning money, someone somewhere is always after money only god could save us from money because god alone does not need money. Is it not ironic we need money at least that's what we are told; To be able to save our own soul they demand ten percent total nonsense So you must keep working and scrambling to have affiliations with the lord because the church stuff seems like a bluff about the lord. That is tough so it is a business like any business your business is to mind your business and get money to handle your business. This delusion is far and wide mister illusion has us running wild we are petrified and disorganized as we take a scuba dive free falling all the while. We are actually mummified alive only god could save us on this ride the irony is it is mass confusion hidden delusion. We are fools rushing in where wise ones fare to go' our destruction is certain because we are uncertain, then our last stance will be to pull the curtain. Nothing is clear until realization gets us there; that gut feeling is unmistakable That's why manipulation has us in a choke hold, as realization has not yet crossed our road' it is different for every one as the road you on forms your opinion All that's important is inhaling and exhaling as we try to navigate and balance. Money has us so corrupt everything we do is so abrupt. Not caring not loving not contemplating on the important things like a kind word or simple smile that could carry us along on our ride. Stuff could be intense, should we be so tense, leaning on the fence might make some real sense before we venture unannounced. Repeating the same old is getting to old, being boxed in is too confining Interpretation could be confrontational it is often a bridge to disruption, as you may not see it as I would or should. Then the perspective destruction hits like a slug, how you see your stuff could clear up your stuff' as that will determine how you tackle the stuff How you hear could make things so clear and you're aware your action is your works. That's why your action speaks louder than your words. If you mean it when you say it, only when you keep it you acknowledge it. Then it becomes full proof some ones word used to be there bond, now it is something that you throw into the pond and run from. Misrepresentation of one self is a fictionalization of one self, sometimes used for deceit in a situation. Starting off wrong always lead you wrong, but right and wrong could coexist like positive and negative. Because of the actuality that one needs the other to be effective. Why is it that for the life ah me I don't get that does that mean only god could be all positive because his power is affirmative. The deeper you go it does not get easier though in every good person is bad person, that's why life is uncertain. Whatever you harbor could actually inspire, motivation comes when benefit comes a compromise could tantalize as you try to analyze. Worldwide combinations work in tandem to create cohesion. There is a time and place for everything, a time to try something and a time to do nothing, because there has to be a time for some observing. There is a reason why change is constant because goodness is not always present. Adjustments transform life this surely is a hell of a life, but you only benefit when you contribute to life. Where there is truth a lie is close by, the cover up is done by infecting the truth with a little white lie.

Sometime truth hurt that is why we continue to work on little things. To create interest in the bigger things that is reusable and valuable when stuff becomes disposable. Then we get in trouble because what you dispose of always seems to be the wrong stuff and must be recouped. Therein lies the proof, if you do not have the skill set you will get upset, continuity is the domination component holds the key to continuity. Having it means getting something continuously available therein lays the fable. The personal guarantee money does that so easily, that commodity is everybody easy pill under the sill. Being number one is only that could be lonely, combinations are popular and you stand to go further with the prop factor. One depends on the other, things are made much easier help and self creates self-help good for a while only for a while. Rejuvenation in motion a deserving action, if the church creates belief that could be a relief, being relevant is convenient that makes sense. Any help is good I would help if I could, but if you say in order to get help I must pay for help because the lord needs my help. Heaven is free there isn't a fee, deluding me will not set you free. God is truth so tell me the truth do not use money as a deceiving fruit. Emotions are vulnerable don't use me as a bundle. Because I stumble and fumble I am also humble don't confuse me to manipulate me. Believing fictitious rubble is trouble from the get go, someone who believe is innocent until proven guilty scholars believed the earth was flat for centuries then they were proven wrong. God want my time not my tide to tidy up my inside, without money a human diminishes without money our lord flourishes. Where money is concerned to the lord it is of no concern because money is earthly the lord is heavenly. What is needed greatly on this earthly realm is of no consequence on the spiritual realm. There is a reason why riches do not get you to heaven. And there is no monopoly that pulls you to the lord. Status is hopeless like endless success on earth is useless, maybe got to be simplicity is the exception, but that's only a perception. Water and oil do not mix one will rise above and one will stay below. Spiritual and carnal is part of that faction that is why there is confusion. Interpretation and consideration should be given throughout the duration. Each individual will have their own opinion at the end of the day. Heaven holds a place for those who pray. It is an in in, but we think it is an out in. Suddenly that disposable commodity money that makes us disposable becomes disposable. What do you know because you know you in trouble when you do not have money on earth; all things possible become obsolete and discrete. The big high becomes a big slide when positions are reversed. Because love is about money and war is about money that is an earthly folly that follows us continuously. Because when you have no money everything is about money. Like a smile is a frown turned upside down, love is war turned upside down; and when you read love backwards it is e vol. When money isn't around, everything is turned upside down, so we are stuck in the wroth that disables most of us, then things start to fester sooner or later it is sure disaster. Some of us admit to being unable and we throw in the towel, only a low percentage of us are the fighters. The rest will probably surrender. The top ten percent controls the bulk of the wealth the bottom percentage is at a disadvantage. So money is about control that got the money will control, domination is control the domination imposes power that is why it causes so much disaster. A taker isn't a giver that is fuel for retaliation, as long as domination is the major option the presence of war will not go on vacation. We will continue to have war on stay cation because the ten percent rule means domination. Many more will have to suffer, many more will have to die, as realization steps in line we will continue to ask why, tell me why as we continue to seek our piece of the pie. Where there is life there will be hope, that thing called hope isn't no joke it could be self-administered by being spoon fed, which makes it feasible and it is surely durable, once it is in place, it has a base which works like faith. When what was given was depleted, it somehow has to be repeated, that's why it is so important and potent, and for every action there is a reaction. Every situation has an occasion because the process is continuous. Relevance will be the focus, what may have been relevant in past times. Has no guarantee as relevant this time, or any other time for a matter of fact. The more things change the more they remain the same. A different outlook does not mean a different in look, what you see when you look all depends on how you look. Someone mind is a major influence, it is the player in the life game, you know it is a game right, a game of survival. There is always a rival to cause a reprisal, someone will not agree with your opinion, so it is ongoing and endless. A sprinter cannot be a good adviser in a marathon and expect to be effective that is logical. If one is broke they cannot be expected to advise on finances, simple logic so what will you say is the rule, that would help if it helps someone to improve, trying is what comes to mind, every time it helps, it helps every time. When you try and it works, right away you realize this isn't a joke. So why do not many more try, there is an underlying lying current called fear, of the unknown, it is sometimes unclear but what is clear, it stalls you like a statue and makes you lifeless like a statue, then you per-sue nothing. Most really fear it could be intimidating because fear remains there is a mist in the air, it exist to scare if you fear. You just remain right where you are and you remain what you are' a statue is anchored as that is its burial. That is clear, fear is a retardant acceleration You will not take a chance, that is not who you are, so far adjustments makes a wealth of a difference. Trying is an achievement in a nut shell, you need it to learn any skill, and you need it to earn your money that is pleasing to anybody. The covering could disguise and misrepresent the inside. The cover story is not the real story, when you open up the flavor is served up then you are covered up. Someone must sacrifice something in order to gain something, because you get out what you put in. That is so interesting, it is magical, some try to get something out without putting out anything that is a fall out, some prefer a hand out, and not a try out Nothing ventured nothing gained your game will remain the same. A statue like looking lifeless situation needs some intervention; sooner or later some [TLC] could enhance. Same old same old soon becomes too old, innovative destroys out dated. Stagnant certainly resonates with dormant. Mobility have the ability of visibility you move freely when you could see clearly, a visionary have the ability of insight, that's the guide for doing it right I would say though, right or wrong is a move you learn from, a right or a wrong move keeps you in tune, no move is not a good move you improve when you move, circulation improves. Money keeps you on the move, you will not be sulking, you will be thinking of something, you will be upbeat and your adrenalin will be flowing, so dormancy won't exist because mobility defeated it. Physically and mentally you are ready to conquer, which is the armor of the conqueror; off course the conquering factor is the monetary factor The domination exerts power and rules all over because of the acquisition factor, a durable useable tool a main stay that possesses like a spirit. Domination is an occupation that dominates like an evil spirit, merciless and careless regardless of status Greed dominates need that's why the needy is ignored by the greedy, being a have not means society cares not, you have nothing to give so society does not care if you live. Only God cares if you live or not; as not to live means you not to give. Only god cares if you exist or not, the difference between God and money are conditions, God love you and I without conditions, another human will love you but there are always conditions. If you are broke not much will work, because you are getting choked trying to get things to work, it sounds like a joke don't it. Only God cares about you before you have made it. Everybody cares about you because you made it, but it is superficial and equivocal; whatever you did replaces you and now represents you at will. Nobody cares about you that are why you are a no body. So everybody could actually care, if there is a dare, I think I am being fare The trick is to be needed, money is always needed, then you get respected and represented, there is something about being wanted. Finding and knowing your skill set is designed to get you set, finding yourself is not easy but you could find yourself somewhat easily. Knowing what works or what you lucky with, will give you some comfort as you feel legit' knowing what is capable of sparking is what will drive you. Challenge yourself when you do not have to, avoid settling if you do not fit in, time will guide you in the interim, ultimately time chooses for you when you do not choose for yourself' or when you become tentative and unresponsive. There is a window a temporary window, that opens for you, as time goes on life goes on then the window closes gradually. Things happen and the blinkers goes on like blinders they keep your focus. We sometimes stumble, on something interesting to us; just like that we are living our dream. Life is a marathon and not a sprint, what impacted in the beginning stays with you to the end, like a moment in time is frozen in time. Many things look so promising in the beginning, but they end up being so disappointing There are consequences for every action and a reaction to an action some call it contemplation. Some call it inseparable oneness on this earthly realm separation from money is a no can do. On the spiritual realm separation from God is a no can do. What do we do, the best we can do, is what a clear conscience, implore us to do. I got a notion on this occasion, that's destined to cause some confusion. Is money synonymous with the world famous mark of the beast; If you will not be able to purchase anything without the mark and you will be left in the dark, am I paranoid or plain old annoyed, as I am confronted with a dominant message, I am being squished like a sausage in a sandwich. Money is stifling me to stillness, I am trying to get it on, but money is bent on making it wrong. Because I was born without a crown does not mean I was destined to be down. Money could be described as selfish, it could also make you selfish, I guess after not having it, I think I could get the fact of one wanting to keep it in tact. Once you get it, you will probably guard it, easily understandable without even a mumble, to impose on it, money gives you authority because it possesses authority, you could gain the whole world though but still lose your soul. You do not want that though, your soul is all you got in your bag pack. Your soul is you, even if you do not know that for a fact, it is truly you. Your soul knows you like your name; it is the one thing that is exclusive to us. That is how karma follows you weather you know it or not, you have to settle your account, hell we have to settle our account. Some say karma do not count, you live once and you die once, so what is the reasoning behind forgiving our sinning, what is sinning isn't it our doing. What is karma isn't it also our doing, so if we did whatever then we should be responsible for whatever, there is no free ride in any life, it is easier to commit and harder to remit But I keep hearing preachers say, ask for your forgiveness and be a witness do not worry the lord will forgive any and every sin, because he died for our sins, but we keep on sinning, will he keep on dying, if we are not trying. We use ten percent of our brain capacity, but still believe we could get off on a technicality, God is loving not stupid and he operates at full capacity daily, so if we are using just ten percent and the lord is at one hundred percent we cannot pull a wool over Gods eyes, even if we try so I wonder why we try. Saying you sorry, is it that easy, to dispose of unwanted sins, isn't that nice. Is it now easier to depose of sins than to commit them Money is being used as a tool to remit them. So money is playing us physically, now it is making a play for us spiritually. The dominance continues, money has a hold on the churches I'm told. In the first place, the lord made everything that was made in six days or six years and he rested on the seventh day, that's what they say but someone is being born every day and someone dies every day and the soul do not dwell with the dead oh well. I do not know more for sure so let's close that door. Money is the kingpin, of use everywhere it is plausible and applicable, Accountability poses no trouble, accompaniment is the action of success, association with money is envious, that is obvious, it activates on having visibility of the subject, ones inner taught could make then a convict, the crime of not having is draining from what is remaining, money now have earthly domination, to our lord it is just earthly destruction, because all the money stays here when we exit, from here on, anything that money could buy would be left like items on a drive by. Money is like words you communicate with, with, money that should be the end of the story. Currently we dictate with money, we dictate because of money, our entire lives is centered around money, some say God want us to prosper, even if it is on the backs of a brother or sister, but thanks to God there is a time period for everything, and change is continuously happening So hope is contagious and has now become famous and we have been banking on hope for centuries, on the returning of the lord, what happened before and after the lord, who was the focus, off course nobody actually knows the lord, so he could already be here, no one alive could connect, there we could all be sleep like, walking zombies in the making, unaware of our surroundings. What in the world is even happening, this life is fragile like a dream and nothing is ever like what it seems. It is a worldwide assumption and off course, there is no manual it is trial and error, emphasizing trying, the key to learning and experiencing anything. Money is the earthly king, trying is the earthly queen, once you try you could achieve far and wide. Independence will build your confidence, money is all right but the lord is right by all, to the lord money is just another insignificant option while to us human's money is the real option. In accepted reality the world is in threefold, you have the first world the world of the haves, the second world the world of those who think they have, then we have the third world, the world of the have not, our existing triangle r concept. Which is self-explanatory the three sides must be connected to be effective, if the concept is not triangulated, it is destined to fail, so believe it or not, the rich needs the poor and the poor needs the rich, with the variable being fairness, a livable wage for honest work anytime that is compromised. The triangulation becomes undone, so although money is king it needs the work to be done, in order for the domination to continue. Desperation is always a deterrent that creates a smoke screen to hinder visibility and clarity. So when we do not see clearly, agreement is in jeopardy, when that happens the order of business becomes a nightmare of business, one side usually compromises, to impede continuity. Money is the jell that makes things work so well, on earth each sphere has its wonder, solar power is another wonder from over yonder, water and fresh air is invaluable hear on earth, humans are here just to try to make it back, to their original home, this is the playing ground, look at how money plays us around, you know because this life is a game, a game of survival and revival. Where we are playing roles, as we stroll towards our real goal, finding ourselves and knowing ourselves, then finding our lord and savior, and contemplating on him, everything comes from him, so even a steer from him could make a world of a difference, in reference to wisdom knowledge and pure understanding. So we will not have to be guessing and be consumed by illusion, who are bent on using tricks, someone mind is vulnerable, as it is flexible to creativity. The mind is imaginative, and it is open to superlatives and comparatives, that's why innovative is massive, it has a built in advantage, because it creates a brand new package, innovation is like creation, the adaption of a notion, to give it traction, and to get participation, you need advertisement, so the money is crucial for arrival and survival, to bridge the gap and pull the slack. When a crack needs to be filled, you already know the drill; I admit money pleases me like I know it pleases you. What am I going to do if there is no money, twiddle my thumb pretend I am dumb, look at time run like a rerun, when there is money everybody is happy, you have mobility and possibility, Working together in perfect harmony, there is no animosity or inscrutability. The accountability is, money answers to nobody, because nobody is bigger than money, we devote our entire working lives, in a quest for earning money. So don't tell me it is not about money, it is only about money, to do things well and to jell, even to feel good like well, keep money in your head, when your taught is money, you cannot help but to feel wealthy, a feeling is important, it makes a good assistant, it helps to guide and drive, while you venture and prosper, faith paid off it is a light, that we sometimes turn off, it is designed to keep us humble, it is only natural for us to stumble, and for us to know it is alright to be not right, that teaches us we need to fight to make things alright, fighting is not necessary brawling, it is a strategy that helps in different capacities. Seize matters for verbalizing, it is exciting, that is all it is, only effective use of what you got, could get you what you really want, the fight is in the dog, not in the seize of the dog, that is where a lot of us go wrong. Life could be a run around, as we try to find our way around, the variable is money, we do everything for the money, that's why the domination is easy, who controls the money controls everybody, the mark of the beast have to be money, what else could control everybody, that's why it is so easy, for Lucifer to devour us, it is like taking candy from a baby, no if or maybe, when you know what somebody wants, you could give them what they want, who give it could take it away any day, per say. With the lord being the word and all that, there is no color to a word or nationality like that. Just reality is always present in simplicity in a word, everyone needs the word and everyone could use words' for expression and satisfaction to bring about normalization. Some go for sophistication, to get satisfaction, the word is the action. God is great as he could relate, truth always takes the cake, the truth could hurt, the truth could choke, it could work and it could work well, because we are looking for instant results, that's how we go wrong, our word is to give and to keep, that's why the word is so deep, there is not much you could give and still keep, that is the way, so anyone could have their own way. The word always lead us as we speak, it always precedes us, where did all this complication come from, the word belongs to everybody, anybody has autonomy, no one owns the word really, but everyone is bound by the word, it was it is it is what it is, the word is all there is, because the word is the lord of host, you could explain anything with the word, you could say anything with a word. Simplification personified is the word you could live by, you will know someone by their words, and people tend to or try to exploit the word. So do not try to confuse the word, to break your word, although it is imaginary, you know what is customary, the word is so powerful it could be positive and negative, a two edged sword that cuts both ways, the user is articulatory and divert-err. The word is free like heaven is free, humans got interested and introduced a fee, so money is for human, only money pleases a human, if nothing else is going right and there is money, a human could be happy, there is no love without money, there is no power without money, there is no activity without money, so money is mobility, and accountability to money, is the ability to use it wisely. A fool and there money is always apart, that does not mean you need to be smart' money has a strategy to always depart. Money is a bridge to the ridge, climbing that hill would need some will, when there seems to be no way, your will is the way to find your way, to be pleasing that's a given, when you could articulate you could translate, if anything is out of range, breaking it down is the word game, silence is so golden that's why the word is the chosen, the word never speaks, and our interpretation is so weak, one tenth is the consent we give, it is at our disposal at will, we are pretending to know what we don't know, risking personal crucifixion which is an addiction, as money is already an addiction, it is just birds of a feather flying together, we stupefy ourselves daily making a mockery of the worthy. The word could full us up, but our cup is over turned. And our hands are always open for money, oh lord I could surely use some more money, the word is the lords and the fullness there of, when we mix spiritual and carnal the resultant will be bacchanal. God is what God is, we all guess who god is, if God is the word, he is the world. He could be found all over the world, he is closer than a brother or a sister. But still we cannot find the lord, with all this intellect we are not willing to take risks, being circumspect we are scared of dying and you know I am not lie in. That's why an intellectual is a casualty to the facility, they will not admit but rather permit uneasiness, the nature of which is well known. Money is the tool of this entire world, to make it you cannot do it without it like those before us. The rich was always the focus, some still want to take the wealth, old habits are still felt, we all die and some cry why, did you have to leave cut and dry, the movie was but for a few minutes, so the parts being acted would be for a few minutes, a minute of fame is what most tend to aim at, but most don't even get that, but the word is down pact, your exit is determined before your entrance is dawning, you cannot cheat your karma, it is you no need to bother. It is the contributing factor, for repeating this over and over. We are coming and going like time, always running to something, what to where to no one can tell you, may be the running is to the money, more lix is in the mix, as you make up the stagger, money leaps even further, money cares not about you or me, it is just passing through being expendable, making us vulnerable, it makes you temporarily comfortable, like a drug, then you want more, the chase becomes continuous, and you lose focus, you become a zombie, that's troubling to anybody. When the word makes you, it is solid standing and you will not be shaky. You could not be blown away easily, but when money makes you and it goes away, you crash and you look like trash, because you feel like trash. It is from the bottom up, steady as a rock, the maker is not a faker, trusting takes some waiting, these days we wanting what we are wanting, sooner is better, from our standpoint, later is greater from the lords standpoint. We trust less and we hope less, so we become hopeless and worthlessness. Hopelessness is uselessness, when you become like this it is a sickness, hope is no joke, that thing really works, it is a bridge to nowhere, when you get there you become aware, around the bend isn't the end, but this is the end thank you till we meet again. I love what I can do with money I do not like what money could do to me. It is a payoff, that makes most showoff, then it is difficult to get off, your dependency is your redundancy, and you end up its casualty. If you give a cookie to a monster, it will shake you down for some milk. You negotiate with money, but you do not risk your life on money. Use it as a tool that is the golden rule' only a fool tries to break the rules. But if you allow it to rule you, then you will be ruled, money only abides by the money rule, who got the money always makes the rules' so they can break them; as they are not bound by them. That is why money rules' it is the go to rule, the mule of the lifting tool. It engages humans and machines working in unison' there is no better solvent to give that ultimate result, as it possess the flexibility to be effective in every community' what a commodity not replicable easily the cream of the crop always awaited unabated. Money has that aura of anticipation, any sacrifice will not be too difficult to make when the acquisition of money is at stake. Look at our life and how it is structured; weather we believe in a higher power or not; our survival depends on making money and without it we perish. This concept must have some originality to it; as I dig deeper my questions are getting steeper, it is told that when you burrow you must pay back' money is the most popular burrowed commodity in any community, you cannot even go before the lord if you have unpaid debts. If you harbor malice in your heart you must get rid of it, that is why it is hard to realize the lord in your heart.

My mind has been relentless in giving me the test, by telling me this and telling me that, having me inadvertently believing which has a possibility of deceiving' then I said to myself go with it just see if you could flow with it' you never know if you don't try it, many fell short because of that habit. I didn't get this and I couldn't get that because I was not focusing like that, this mind of mine has been giving me hints like a print, you should try this, why don't you try that, nothing could happen if you don't try to make it happen, you can find out things just by trying things, doing things will just validate things and validate the doer who will be delegated and designated originator, being the starter, so a trier is anyone from anywhere with a dream that is unclear until realization makes it clear, the operative word or the variable should be stressed on like a mantra, the try is the cry of the trier, try and try, authentication ah waits to embrace you, around the corner, the new word term innovator and the old term trier, are intertwined, you can hit rewind as you unwind, trying precedes innovation if you fail to try you fail to innovate, it is a mistake you don't want to make, a try is worth consideration in this mind game, now I get it and I like it, to determine if I possess the characteristics of getting ahead, grit true grit fits, it keeps showing up none stop like the hand of time, embracing the nonstop sign on a nonstop ride' ticking away bringing in the new day, leaving the old day to roll away, I am inundated at the bottom trying to get a grip, my mind set is what will get me set for success, some times of course that could mean hard times but I will not have it any other way, articulation is my chosen way of entering into the conversation. I must first think it, I need to think I can before I can make a run, if I do not then I cannot, mind power keeps the balance it must be manifested within and projected outwards in order to have a forward movement, conceivably possibilities could be endless but if you do not have access it would be useless, a lot means a lot and a little could mean a lot only if your hand is in the slot' many want a lot but they want to sacrifice not, you only stand a chance with a ticket in your hand' as variation is the instrument of consent, without it you screwed that is the golden rule and we must abide. Success is usually the express train, that nonstop train that does not wait for your claim to fame, so you are always playing chase that is why the mind power is so crucial, it drives the point home, perseverance means deliverance you could only deliver if you keep at ah, but finding it is the magic, most never find that factor, imagine being bug down by other factors, but it is what it is. Venturing changes what it is, it is an exclusive club where anyone is welcome, anytime is welcome, anticipating an outcome, something from nothing is always something, the unexpected nature captivates the human nature, maximizing surprising, that could be so enticing, it is another attribute that can contribute to the tribute, doing your do could be good for you, something could be discovered that could prove you are a natural, in this mind game the real game is finding yourself' in order to satisfy yourself. Asserting yourself is bringing importance to yourself, you must first believe it then anyone else will be able to believe it' so you teach people how to treat you, just as you teach you how to treat you, so there is a method to the act of madness' any differing will be sadness when you fall short of your gladness. You are your mind and your mind is you, it showcases your ability by making ya own up to accountability' you cannot do that without acceptability, so your mind power is your super power, why not exploit it and discover it is worth it, someone said it is the mind is a terrible thing to waste' I endorsed that statement with haste, because of what I went through those changes were really true' there is nothing like frank talk to number one because you cannot hide from number one, as you mirrored you remembered your view is authentic' with all the illusion taking place these days, you will be sure you are not on a ride or you are not being taken for a ride, so your pride will be on a high, as everything will be cut and dry, seems so simple but unusually simple. When I say to myself I got game, is it me or my mind playing a game on me' as I project this confidence, is it me in reference or does my mind seek that endorsement' could one be separated from the mind and could one be separated from the brain' that is not likely like being aloft or are they intertwined' this mind powerful mind makes its mark every time, as it possesses leadership and following qualities' coming to think about it that is a universal quality, anyone one could be a leader but you must first be a follower. I'm thinking the lord made that as a standard, to invite harmony and to project normalcy as leaders rise and fall normally, continuity must prevail as the world will not stop to acknowledge someone flop' as everyone has the option to rise but it will take a try, opening uncharted territory' some prefer to not be a trail blazer but just stay a trailer, as most have not yet realized there inner potential' the tail end is heavier as the tail is wagging us instead.

This is not about anybody else, it is good to acknowledge one self, the mind is just about one self, it was said and well said, a mind is a terrible thing to waste, tap into the mind any mind at any time, there will be a discovery that warrants recovery, we all dismiss hunches in bunches, as part of our daily routine, most things are dismissed if they do not fit in our little mix, so we are voluntarily boxed in, self-inflicted and system inflicted, making us the victim, but the default is not our fault, it was built in, anticipating a voiding. The brain is playing second fiddle to the mind all this time, because the responsibility of the mind is so much greater' you could contain the brain but to the mind it is an impossibility, like trying to contain air it is an obvious impossibility, sometimes we are stock between a rock and a hard place' having to entertain the concept of two evils being a moron or accepting the act of an oxymoron, either way you will get dab like taking a jab but the hurt will be temporary like a humans memory, as we are curtailed by our own memory and we are deceiving ourselves which is called insanity' if we are bent on repeating the same and expecting a different result more insanity, or like holding on to something rotten and saying to yourself it is better than holding on to not ten, insanity personified I cannot quantify or even qualify. The mind game is like the money game, same concept in a different respect, as the variable is the illusion' natural confusion, so it is pointless to get restless and reckless' but we know the mind loves the taste of revenge, even if the brain is beckoning you to go another way, it loses every time as the intangibles in life has a way of overriding the tangibles' the pull of the unknown mystifies as it tantalizes' leaving you shaken up like after an episode of a hiccup, seeing is believing and not seeing is deceiving especially if there is a sounding. By golly you will not be jolly hearing a sound with nothing in sight will bring on fright that is right' a natural reaction on such of an occasion. Illusion shines through like a laser with cutting edge capabilities assimilating every and anything in its path, when you least expect it creeps up on you then there is nothing you could do but oblige' as your hands is already tied as you made that commitment in the moment, trying to make it a teachable moment to be able to learn something from the mistake' the sense of surprise deters us every time, as we go on different detours changing our life experience forever. Everyone is on a road that is starkly different to the one they envisage, that is why each and every one of us is a victims of our circumstance' as an animal could only graze where it is tied, excuse the animal analogy. We got to work like animals to get by anyway as our way is our downfall. As soon as someone lets there guards down they will be pull down, as we treat each like animals anyway' on any given day an act of kindness is construed as an act of weakness, trusting in another human is busting in another human' the heart is being played like a toy until you are strengthen from your experience, the illusion takes you low down and realization lifts you high up' so the actual strength comes from within, as soon as you realize you did not die and you are still alive all you could do is try to strive' as accepting defeat is counterfeit and not spendable so it is not dependable, so you withdraw within yourself to gain the required strength to try again' at the end of the day all one could do is just try again. The enemy is illusion that is my conclusion no one is off limits or immune I could safely presume' as everybody is consumed in their own situation, survival is the only step to change your hand' as only if you survive could you thrive and not continue to be controlled by the hive. Like having something precious in your hand' only it is in a dream the illusion have you converted at that point you will be believing in anything, as it is so easy to derail us and thus degrade us by tinkering with our focus' a simple taste could make us strip to the waist, a strange face could take us on a detour forever, the myth of the mind is impossible to confine' the brain is powerful but is easily manipulated by the mind, just as the heart is relative and is also held hostage by the mind' so it is not unusual for the head to go wrong or for the heart to go wrong, being under the influence of the master mind. As it is the thing holding the controlling strings deceiving and impeding us at will, not many better yet not any have free will' we just play our part then depart. As this movie continues the guessing continues only the try could give us a tie, but if we could only strive to try we could release that tie. Moment to moment life continues to happen with highs and lows, our dream is to have more highs than lows so our highs could help us pick up our lows to make things work' as all the examples we have of the stables around us are continuous, time is continuous the same sun has supplied that solar energy to us' so this world is obviously continuous but I do not want to open a can of worms, because it will mean something continuous happening like going and coming' as not everyone is down with it we will try to avoid it this time around, but in the time being feel free to use your imagination for satisfaction.

The mind is my highway surely it loves to play it is what paved the way to find ways daily, maybe each moment is a teachable moment, try to embrace your moments they are a dime a dozen and prone to be forgotten, if highlighted one could be delighted like a child grabbing things pulling things tripping over things falling down and getting up trying things none stop, there is hope for the trier a natural assembler as life is put together, all the concepts and simple aspects are separate and scattered waiting to be put together by a trier, the real game is putting the pieces together in a way that they would be workable and be applicable, which would ultimately be equitable this game is for real with the real feel you know what the real deal is, it is life you taught you were playing for one brief moment then you get a reality check this is for real, I am grown so I need to make a life of my own so I need to get things to do my own thing the mind power have already kicked in, money buys you anything a job gives you money, get a job and you in the thing, the goal is to achieve success so you do not want to regress or to regret, I do not know of anyone one who wants to be nothing but you could earn nothing by doing nothing because nothing from nothing leaves nothing that is where and when your mind power goes into overdrive and begin delegating to the lead off runner your brain to get things going showing, there is a potential for something positive happening negative is nothing happening, planing is always satisfying it is the prelude to something happening, anticipation is a positive action like participation being involved in or with something could be invigorating the mind is instrumental to making that happen being a worker as it is it will get you working, mind power powers all others; a progressive mind is a progressive life because your mind controls your life although your life is a rental temporarily fronting as your own so is the mind because all we really own is our soul in this life and it is being manipulated by our mind for most of our life it isn't right but what else is new. We are doing it to ourselves by wanting more than we need, it used to be that we catered to our needs period and our wants was just window dressing, now the roles have been reversed and things have gotten worse welcome to the bottom less pit scenario nothing is ever enough the more we see the more we want at least it simplified one major concept what is success it is just major excess, more than we will ever need or want to be blunt. Our mind is powerful that is wonderful it could lead us to the bountiful so our mind is just giving us what we want, we just have to show our mind the direction we want to go and it will get us there, we all know that if we buckle down we usually get things done, as our mind is the faster transporter. Look around you what you see are real manifestations of a lot just filling spots and what not, know it or not we all got to make it up as we go or else we are going to be a no show, this is actually a personal show to let us know we got to get on the go just to show, our mind lets us know if we try anything we could find out anything, imagine I am finding out something from just trying not being taught or pampered up I am actually getting fired up charting new territory, I may not be legit but I am too legit to quit because a mind is a terrible thing to waste needless to say my mind has been helping me to keep up the pace in this race, the survival race everyone needs a base to prepare for the chase we are all starting on different levels and we must create our own bevels to attack barriers that will keep confronting us hypothetical or physiological in the wave of reality and virtual reality ultimately, we must create stability in order to be taken seriously, the mind is actually for real the power it has is the real deal, giving me the real feel telling me this and that withstanding and understanding it will come together as long as you do not become a quitter I know that situations differ and stuff will get stiffer, look around you theirs altercations all over, a quitter never wins and a winner never quits you keep on hanging on like a cling on because it is all about holding on, repetitious could be contentious it could cause you to get furious as long as you do not lose your focus it is acceptable like possible, it is all in the journey because the destination is the journey what happens along the way is what helps you to find your own way, where there is a will there is a way by the way you learn the right way from going the wrong way, little hitches and glitches propel you to future fixes that is why you stick to your vision of trying things how you start out differs from how you close out, information gathered even if it was haphazard is what is required for future intervention, the conversation is continuous, explaining could easily be contentious, adjustments are also necessary believe me no one is ever right on, the long and short in compromising is it strengthens understanding it helps you to discover your inner power so you know you could absorb more a lot more like wanting to say something but not saying it and like wanting to do something but not doing it, passive aggression is harnessed aggression that does not mean it is not aggression, the aggressive will get successive bites of the apple of life, while being passive do not exactly get you massive but it is all collective and cohesive, incorporating spirituality is positively appealing but it is an in in, something we misinterpret as an out in because everything comes from within this entire operation comes from within. That is why there are so many misinterpretations because of mere misunderstanding; different people see things in different ways every day. One word so one god, made up words so made up gods, distorted interpretations creating unrealistic misconceptions sad will be our portion if we do not get the notion and get in motion, our relation to the word is the only option because the only thing we could all give and still keep is our word so words are like rental property, you could use them all your life and you will never own them for life that is deep, but no need to deprive yourself of sleep if only we could get a peep as we hit that deep sleep when enlightenment is for keeps, Lucifer have us so distorted and disoriented, we do not even know if we are coming or going, everything is right here we are also right here but we are so unaware, convenient to the trick star bumping us off course of course, to begin with illusion is creating confusion delusion at every junction the church isn't a viable option, it is also on the run and tied up in the delusion heaven is free but you must pay to get free they are interested in you as long as you could tide, the mind game is far and wide they are pulling you in with the tiding tide' it is going to cost us ten percent of whatever we earn to have an affiliation with them, it is like someone selling something that does not even belong to them, the last time I checked the lord wants me to spend ten percent of my time living for him and reflecting his light day and night so maybe someone might be inspired by my deeds because my actions speak louder than my words because it is easier to manipulate my words, I only used the term him just to convey realism because we do not get the word being made flesh for actual tangibility purposes, the flesh being made word works because we are unable to see beyond the flesh, I actually believed that white photo with the hand on the heart was actually that of Jesus, so half of my life was a delusion on the wrong focus, I to could not get the concept of the word being made flesh, another aspect of the mind and its power I was told that picture was that of Jesus and I believed that and my mind took that and ran with that, so what it look like is, we believe on our own so accepting or rejecting is our doing once that is established our mind pushes it to make sure the job has been actually accomplished, another major aspect of the mind is a default when we as individuals fail to act or do not want to act, or are confused about acting our default steps in and fill the gap, that will be steep our mind never goes to sleep so less sleep could extend our potential appeal. Grit has a grip on grabbing it, that it factor is a major factor; it is a combination of realization and the act of perseverance. That gives you the assurance to make it, backing you up like an insurance policy that is the policy, because being gritty and witty is actually imperative. To be competitive simple means competing, a collaboration between the try and the factor' giving you the try factor. like we are capable at any time to perform on a dime' but the mind has us on lock down, it only responds when bacon to, like an opportunity waits for you to embrace it' then it carries you through, so this notion of opportunity knocking' could be majorly misleading I know sometimes you get a gut feeling that you cannot help but perusing, each individual gets the realization in different ways and each mind works in different ways' as we are all at different stages of this game, we never play the same; the mind power turns on the machine inside, relating the fact there is an upside to our down side' some lay dormant unaware of what is there, so they cannot help but be blown away' like dust in a desert nothing else really make sense, introduce an additive like water and you get a makeover' something solid begins to form so something has been reformed, suddenly there is a new reality and stuff begins to pop up' the mind power is a confidence builder and one little spark could start a big fire, the try is the high you could get high on a try as if the lord is saying just try' even if you have to cry, after wards just try. We all exist in our own reality and because of that we become our own casualty' as some have everything and they do nothing with, others have nothing and they do everything with it' that taste test when you get your beak wet that door opening is critical and pivotal, you just have to think it and you can do it, that is mind power spinning on a dime, some have the fight within and some seem to not, introduce the mind power and it changes that' call it the controller you will not be out by far, believing you could achieve goes a long way to achieving' the mind test is never useless as it could be tricked to put you in the mix, if you want to try doing something you won't usually do the result might startle you it is all meant to inspire you. On a level playing field to start out, most cannot relate to that, something somewhere is always out ah whack' we are handicapped with constrains, but we got to take it to the game, in a best case scenario, things are not always so but as we all know things are made up as we go, some always have an advantage over others, where you finish is the big deal, most times it is the big steal, it should not leave you diminished, only then you will be able to feel accomplished, our mind is notorious because it could lead us both ways, truth that will not exist without the driver our mind the changer. A major denominator in this fix ah up ah, the pieces are scattered all over and we got a life time to put things together, when we make an effort our mind gets focused. The push is in us, it's built within us' but when dormancy becomes normalcy it changes our policy, we are so into winning at all cost we actually loose something with constant winning, reality is not like that' so balance gives us a whack, that is the concept of correction balance is an insurrection without it the prevailing law will be unsure, like the law of gravity is designed to keep you grounded, without it there will be a lot of floating around' like a link in a chain everything has limited gain in the learning process, he express concept works but it does not pay handily because learning is done gradually, earning is done gradually, appreciating is done gradually and living is done gradually, that is why realization only comes gradually like wisdom knowledge and clear understanding' experience is a great teacher but innovation is the principal, why is mind power behind that' because it is mind over matter.

When you dig in there is no quick fixes, a sprinter in a marathon will be gone before long because that concept is residing in the wrong place we should be more into doing and that is simply trying, finding out is just trying out we often seal our own faith by not showing up, for our own date on top of the plate, that diamond is our pivotal station the launch needs to be packing a punch to be authentic or you get no lunch the one with the punch will be having your lunch, our mind wants us to try it, it is incumbent on us to try if we do not try we just lie to ourselves and deprive us of our independence, then our confidence disappears like the wind on the skin you feel it so you know it exists but you could never see it or touch it tangibility is none existent, we are cutting ourselves short from the beginning, as we are programed to believe from the beginning that winning is everything, when it is trying that is everything, winning and losing is comparable because the difference is often miniscule a looser only loose when they become a quitter every winner was once a looser, perseverance bridges the gap and packs the crack to get you over the hump so you will not slump and go belly up, over on your back for lacking the tact to impact change the general act and a constant act that is typical and universal the mind game never stays the same once you make up the stagger, the direction and concept changes, so you are always on the edge of the well digging in to sink in because realization is a positive action once you get it you could never forget it suddenly with this new found attribute you could pay tribute to bearing and advancing the use of the fruit as the mind continues to make roots into the very fabric of our being. Sometimes deceiving us into believing what we are not detecting' case in point this virtual vocation apparatus you know for a fact that you did not go anywhere because you did not even pack after that experience our mind is telling us that we had a vacation when we know fully well all we had was a stacation, so manipulation is an ongoing and a viable option awaiting implementation extending the confusion like the roots of any tree crossing and reinforcing to prevent falling and intruding thus impeding the progress of another, isolation or being confined to a location is sometimes purposeful and helpful when you are trying to be forceful and engage your inner useful, silence is golden and powerful while you prepare to be resourceful the inner thinker is the dispenser of the needed answer the calm after the storm a welcome reform to conformity and uniformity, atrait that is complementary to seemingly any individual with an objective, the bond is an incentive which works as a corrective, persuasively is nothing more than a maybe there is always a pull to rancor, love and hate continues to affect our faith when you love someone you tend to think about them all the time and if you hate someone you also think about them all the time, so love and hate relates like positive and negative relates, thinking about is actually interesting one is no good without the other so neither could generate power on its own so the combination is an abomination but look at the resultant positive action throughout this nation, am I on to something or what love and hate needs to exist and they need each other to exist then why are we all bent out of shape trying to eliminate hate no wonder that is a mistake, with all the scholars in the field none are able to muster in a deal we must individually get on our knees, the roots benefit from sustenance anywhere we could benefit from sustenance anywhere, Christians and Muslims are eliminating each other because of distorted thinking I am presuming that interpretation have a malfunction that causes some dysfunction, with our level of articulation understanding is still none what is the relationship with the mind and the sprit there is no better server a career servant is mind power a personal computer literally the stabilizer of this reliable machine put your mind to doing something and everything changes, chances are you will get it done the mind is the fight in everyone that is why the seize color or creed of someone is irrelevant someone mind is all that is relevant it could be prevalent to discover your mind and keep it engaged every time a mind is a terrible thing to waste like time is a terrible thing to waste even while you are asleep your mind is taking a peep. Something potentially deep with the capabilities of making you weep will be on the mind radar while you slumber. If only we could tap into that fountain, the mountain will be within our reach' and we will not have to operate on chained and missing the mark over and over, as we keep going around like a go around, all we are getting is our giddy on. We could eliminate this thirsting for knowledge it is right here already there it is just that we are unaware, the equipment was installed and is in place all ready to compile data' but so far it is gathering dust and what not, fungus is flourishing out of control because we are not plugged in if we could connect and eliminate that disconnect, more and more I am realizing we need the lord to put these pieces together instead of operating off the hook everything would go right instead of most things going wrong because the knowledge we seek is giving us the creeps I am thinking the mind could help we could lead it and help ourselves in the process' we have an idea of what is right and what is wrong or do we, you could fool me not withstanding distortion is rampant that is so apparent, no wonder we are having difficulty finding our own self so how could we find another, that is a bummer but the mind is a runner it is difficult to hold on, stilling the mind will control it fine, something like that takes time we devote our life time to another, there is hardly any room for another the survival app or the cash trap, without it we are strap, if it was not for that we probably would be able to accomplish the fact which is stilling the mind, the act of a still mind makes you compact that is what we live for, if we could only calm it we could get on and ride it, because working with it is critical, finding the answers we seek will take a tireless, only perseverance could convey our reverence towards seeing the light if we could achieve that there would be no need for this continuous disappearing act' for some reason we think we could make it without the lord so we try to do it without the lord then we realize it is all about the lord but we are stubborn and we hardly respond so that compounds our misery definitely we relate to what we can see, we could relate only to tangibility because we have the ability to touch it, the word we cannot touch have the ability to touch us, that word is the word of words, that word is god who is worthy to be called the holy one so we muffle words and baffle ourselves in a quest to manipulate, ending up deceiving ourselves they even created a fictitious face for the lord, I grew up believing what was so wrong now I am trying to turn it around with many stumbling blocks all around. Realizing tangibility does not possess the ability to comprehend intangibility my mind had the capability all along of helping me to turn this all around but I didn't know better my light was not turned on. I was like any other unaware of what was here or there all along. This word rules supreme over every being, the word created everything there is and was, every human knows words except the supernatural word' we could never own words we could only express words, it is the breath that we breathe to be real and have a feel, without the fresh air let us make it clear we will not be able to exist here. So we need air for expression the word gave us that permission to exist in this organization of communication, self-expression is a bridge understanding is the ridge put them together and they would get you over yonder and on the way to have your say' they are reusable and fully capable of helping you find your way in this concrete jungle just to mingle and to handle the order of business which is your business, without the word there are no words expression will be a joke sit back and let it work the word is the works theirs is no existence without it no moments or improvements without it no changes without it the word is just above it all and above us all like a permanent cloud, the mind is a good servant the word is the greatest master but we try to manipulate the word and thus the master, it is insanity we have lost our sanity no wonder our own mind cannot bear to be around us it rather run away and play instead of volunteering to stay focusing and pray to be able to break this repetitious cycle of wanting more than we could handle we don't ever get the concept of enough, we are gluttonous and out of sorts, the mind could stable us by corralling us, but we have to find a way where their seems to be no way we the help must help the helper our mind otherwise it will be continuous disaster this has been ongoing for a while now I don't know how long all I know it has been to long being repetitious is actually precious it helps us to focus and serve our purpose, the word is waiting patiently for us to call on it voluntarily, but there is a process for any kind of success, being relentless and having patience could demobilize you realistically, how many of us have patience these days the mantra is right now right away like yesterday as soon as possible, like fools we are rushing in uncertain that could be pain staking the wise will contemplate because that will be more appropriate the road test to success is believing even if things are not exactly working, that is a real parameter around the perimeter the difference between success and failure is often miniscule, so failure should not be ridiculed as a rule. Being a failure at something could be cruel, so close but yet so far. Success and failure is close like a brother and sister one more try or one kind of belief could have resulted in relief' the mind could have brought about that relief there would have been no giving up or no giving in if the mind had bit in, the power of belief is mind related without the mind invested in the situation it will be over rated to stress on the power and influence of the mind, its capable of misleading if it is not in it whole heartedly the fact of the matter is the mind is above matter if something should matter the mind could make it a factor if there is apathy there will be energy. Ambiguities are usually the enemies double meaning could be mind boggling why or why not is in effect just to get you set for the test any surprise is a test especially if you are caught and your feet isn't set yet do not forget things only matter when the mind make it matter someone or something matters not if the mind do not want to acknowledge that some are delusional and become confrontational someone matters because it is earned or given but it is not a given, the mind could make sense out of nonsense because your mind is smarter than your two sense, your mind could make you think you been somewhere when you know you been nowhere it could also propel you to get somewhere even if you are unaware weather you could get there the mind is our engine that is always running it could take you site seeing without planning, so ride shot gun and you will be on an incredible run, this marathon isn't easy to fathom, it takes a while to figure this out by the time you get it figured out it is time to forget it the mind is in control and the heart also controls our emotions so the mind controls the matter of life and the heart controls the emotion in life the mind is our personal computer and the heart is our human factor that combination is the human one leans on the other and the earth bridges the gap giving the human some tact for a fact, how we interact with other humans is vital for our salvation basically we should respect another human and treat them like we would like to be threated when we hurt a heart we hurt our heart whatever good we do for someone we actually did for ourselves so when we genuinely help others we genuinely help ourselves that's why what goes around comes around because all it is a go around on each go around you discover as you recover from your last go around by the time we have this figured out go figure our time has almost run out, without an actual manual it is all about the trial, it is instinctive to be active that in itself is massive being passive renders you inactive' the go getter makes things better for themselves and other selves. What is on the shelf stays on the shelf if not activated it could remain aggravated. That goes for the undecided doing nothing about something says something about nothing' it could be that you are not interested or your mind have not been offered an incentive or a bribe, persuasion is an art form inciting someone to perform strategically, our mind have the ability to make that a reality' it is just part of the domain so you will continue to remain on radar, interaction is a prelude to action or perspective action the mind is powerful in inducing action this revolution of action is all mind related the fact that most of us want more than we need is mind driven the fact that nothing is ever enough is totally mind related stuff. Seeing is believing and feeling is believing when those two combine there is no unbelieving our mind could back us into a corner at will we do not even have the free will our mind gives the order so technically we just follow orders but that is the general order the word is the world order although it might seem to be other than that this entire world is pretentious no wonder why so many situations are suspicious it is a general cover up to get on top most are unhappy with what they got because it miraculously deviates from what permeated in the first place' individuals think they have control the illusion of delusion is just dealing us different hands all we can do is the best we can when we are in a confused state the decision we make could be described as a mistake, not the take we would make under normal circumstances, once it is made by you it is you we all have to own up to our doings although persuasion came from the mind action we must own up because it was recorded as our action no one else is or should be responsible for our personal action because only us are responsible even for our in action that is what defines us that is what represents us that is what is presented when the focus is us that is our karma, our karma is our doing everything we do anything we do even if our mind influenced us to, so our mind and our karma is us just us so we are responsible for us just us because we came alone and we are leaving alone theirs is something special about being alone it is only and it could sometimes be lonely but accomplishments achieved alone are the most special in the entire world like learning to learn and learning alone like making up your mind to try and trying alone like justifying something alone like decision making which should always be done alone because when or if there are consequences they will be better handled alone because every individual is different every mind is different there is nothing like a typical mind. But there could be typical kinds and identical finds love is a special kind if you are the tolerating kind giving and taking is what we call compromising. By so doing a lot more get done and more get going so compromising is inviting and enticing giving a solution to infighting an agreement is important because no agreement is poignant to progression could an agreement be made without the intervention of the mind I think not phycology or the study of the mind will not allow that because it is hands on, the mind is beckoning us on with its quick response like the controller always concealed on the inside allowing other subjects to front as the controller, extrapolation or an educated guesstimate' is our life long occupation by trying different things we put ourselves in a realistic position, to find the ideal position we are all victims. Our individual circumstances are pitiful as we never get what we really want because we are not that important under normal circumstances because our mind is arranging everything that we are doing if we only show some sort of initiative that will ultimately be to our advantage it seems like our mind controls us on earth so our soul is burdened with all these decisions because every decision is consequential our soul is that light within that shines through and it gives us that glow which forms that halo but over the years it has been burdened with dirt and filth so it cannot illuminate and rise to its potential being, shackled with this armor of dirt and scum that keeps us grounded and dumfounded so taking flight is unexpected the extra weight is daunting so nothing major is expected from us we are all relegated to the minor league because the great deceiver has got our number he knows that the mind is into play and excitement, so Lucifer the destroyer knows how to provide that so we are hanging on his string playing to his tune and playing by his rules so this game of life on earth is a tossup you only have half of a chance to make it because we are running from behind from day one only the word could give us a word to defy the odds in this world with all that power the great deceiver possesses it is all negative the word is the only positive and interactive force to save us from ourselves, imagine on average we are actually using just ten percent of our brain capacity and we are creating such havoc if another ten percent was to be utilized we could be tantalized as if we haven't fantasized enough, the need of someone always had precedence over their want, is the mirror image now dictating to the image insanity it is unrealistic and almost impossible, so I guess all things are possible is more than just a quotation it is now a literal action that is open to participation 'another diversion of the mind and its action. The root controls the tree so the root is the tree anything that comes from the tree must be thankful to the root for up keep and stability because steady means ready. Ready to try and ready to ride ready to jump aside to save your hide' jump through hoops as you are being thrown for a loop, ending up on your feet and being cat like is your desired resultant' ready to fight is an antidote against defeat, a feat accomplish by preparing in anticipation of something happening the brain have that power to decipher' that thinking power that is above many others, to think makes you independent so you are not dependent thus making you confident knowing you are capable of performing adequately on your lonesome which is like awesome, having interdependence isn't ideal but it does a good deed by meeting individual needs, I think we refer to it as compromising we all have our little sticking points or that proverbial breaking point' by contemplating you could achieve a smaller percentage of what you originally wanted, so you along with an unlimited amount of others in any combination could coexist and resist the temptation of noncompliance, then we have adjusting a major factor in this life or any life as a matter of fact, what might seem to be so wrong on the surface could be transformed to being so right with some common adjustments just another branch of the powerful mind it is above matter as some like to say it is mind over matter, if anything matters the mind is what matters where ever you want to get to the mind could get you there' all because there is no better promoter and controller, the mind could get you in and out and around about it is a good leader and a good follower' because any good leader was a good follower you learn in order to know and you bring what you know, another obvious quality of the mind is dictating I guess that is right up there with the best it is life long and it prolongs continuously, seriously their isn't much that the mind does not have control of, to suggest that the mind isn't in total control will be an anomaly, a deviation from the norm or normalcy thus creating ab normalcy' going against the grain accepting pain has always been a way to gain, because we have all heard it, no pain no gain, so accepting pain have always been a way to gain but off course we all prefer no pain, so the only way of accepting some pain is to be motivated to confront some pain so preparation will be all important off course if you fail to prepare you must prepare to fail theirs no other avail to prevail' disregarding existing restraints is an experiment of assertivness which is best when done in all fairness, defying the odds shouldn't be odd but they do in the dare makes everything clear. Mediocrity is so out of here because the mind is a natural driver and pusher anything you put your mind to do, you probably could do that means something, even if nothing means nothing and nothing from nothing leaves nothing, the pusher behind us all is free to all. It is activated by the will off all, like the proverbial heaven which is free to all as long as you can adapt and wont crack, because you will be attacked by those holier than thou regardless of what is being said or fed' interpretations will always be wide spread because no mind is typical that is certainly pivotal in this reality, I am forced to phrase this like that because supposedly our reality isn't the only reality, that should be acceptable if virtual reality is acceptable, anyone who pushes themselves could compete and alter their defeat because winning and losing could be one more dip in the pit to avoid the glitch, so many give up on stuff thinking that they do not have enough of what it takes to be enough' so many of us are sealing our own faith making that age old mistake by not taking what they are given. Always preferring somebodies reality as opposed to their own, because you do not always get what you want, you must embrace what you get' it might be good to cherish what you have because you could perish thinking of what you do not have' someone said a bird in your hand is worth two in the bush anticipating the trouble you might encounter acquiring another, coming to think about it what we call our mind isn't our own it is another muscle on lone to us like our heart and lungs and others, because our soul is all we own in this world and we have the manipulation factor in common, because of our needs and wants our soul is over burdened by what we want and even need, we are all grounded by our need and want of and for money, it gives us energy and mobility because we are all grounded without some money, our mind seems to understand that concept, is it the system commanding more or is it us demanding more' it does not matter to our mind it will just bug us down some more, so our load is going to get heavier, karma endless karma, more cravings more doings more and more needing and more wanting and none of that stuff could accompany us that is rough, but in this western civilization we are stuck in that one life to live stuff, so we are not coming back and Jesus died and saved us from our sins, so we do not have to pay for it again so Christians are special, there are no consequences for their actions, I am having trouble with that but in first peter 3-18 and revelation 5-9 also in romans 4-25 basically resolves me from my responsible then why do I feel uneasy, is my mind misleading me like virtual reality, I know that god will not lie. So how could I get this clarified, it surely blowing my mind I could chance it but that will not solve it, kicking the can down the road does not mean it is off the road, all it means is it is outa my way or my thought temporarily I prefer permanently. This mind has been truthful as a result I look forward to being fruitful. The mindset is what gets you set to take the test' as many have discovered we are not ready and surprises are plenty, so we need time to digest and to vent as we lament our predicament' this is not what I planned: why did I even plan, I do not like what is in my hand' I rather what is in somebody else hand, from then on it will be a down slide' as you cannot rise with what does not belong to you, many have found out that is true so there is no other way through. In the interim though it might seem that it does not matter, some might even seem to prosper but mister failure awaits yah around the corner, because what hasn't met you yet hasn't passed you yet' it is imperative that you never forget it, in the midst of making your huge strides comes an unforeseen detour that surprises you as it shakes you to the very core, making you unsure and it shatters your confidence' guaranteeing unforced mistakes to take place. Everyone knows the deal with making mistakes, they are never welcomed' people have an aversion for making mistakes, even though one could learn from a mistake' but there is more comfort from not making one, when we get into that comfort zone 'we get into that dormant state where interruption is a say it isn't so. When I feel acne is it me or my mind' I know my mind is notorious for overriding decisions sometimes, as I know it is a two way street. I know this for sure without knowing for sure by getting these inclinations I could do this or that if I try, could that be the mind power or just the try power, what is the balancing factor' equilibrium comes across as a conundrum Me and my mind have these heart to heart chats all the time, I will say this it is informative' the mind could run with a simple taught if we stress on it long and hard enough, accentuation is prominent like a punctuation' it stands out like a sore thumb or a middle figure, one thing is for sure projection is tenable To make a long matter a short matter' it only matters if it is the heart of the matter and if it could withstand the stress test, yes everything goes through the stress test' as our mind gives us the stress as it puts us through the test, you could do better but take a rest as you reset. There is always more work to be done to keep changing the outcome, change comes with the push, give up on the push and you will get squish like a squid' whatever it is has to be continuous like a heartbeat. Without it we are all dead our dreams are dead our hopes are dead and our purpose will be dead, then the mind will be left without a head to reside in which is uninspiring' a wasted mind is a wasted life because it makes all the difference in this here life. The power is the tower as it pivots and hovers over forever. Just a simple taught makes a huge difference. As we need to think to inflict a sense of duty' as the carry the load for us and those who cannot speak, I often wonder about the animals there brains lies dormant' some of them possess all that power but not a word will they be able to otter, I would not of wanted to be in that situation' communication and expression is life's major solution, I would be dumbfounded and I would feel intimidated, not to be able to express having to suppress and digest I guess we are bless, this time around as the players change but the game remains the same' as the breeze blows and time goes we follow on and life goes on, it seems like everything in life is continuous' the moon and the stars are light years away and light years old, the sun mister solar with all that power has been shining forever' our master the creator seems to have a track record of forever, that is the deal with authentic' top quality so it has durability with the possibility of wit standing the test of time. If we were retrofitted with what we needed to get by that could be considered as our brain you would think. So it does not matter maybe what we call it, what gives us the ability to make any decision is the brain and we already know it is a muscle, so use it or lose it, but it is twofold' it leaves you alone if it is left alone like an opportunity, but if you indulge the brain it will indulge you and if you do not know something you just don't know, as knowledge is like money once you get a little you want more and money is never enough so is knowledge' the taste ignites the haste and you can no longer wait or be passionate, that is the price that is paid for being late' gradual is replaced with astronomical, a mere drink becomes a gulp like consuming pulp. I a nut shell the brain is a good friend and also your worst enemy' if we stay within our needs it is a good friend, but if we exceed our wants that you do not want' our brain opens the flood gate that later drowns you in regrets, more have a way of wanting more, as birds of a feather have a tendency to flock together' more and more it is becoming painfully evident, humans are unable to have enough we cannot be satisfied' it seems unnatural but it is actual as long as you indulge the brain nothing will ever be the same again. It is the gift of plentiful that puts you on the road of bountiful, but endless becomes useless because after a time it is actually senseless, like those who were able to amass huge amounts of wealth in their life time' at the end of their time most have to give it away, as they cannot spend it anyway' not acknowledging some of those who were instrumental in helping them acquire it in the first place. Some have too much others have not much, how come this much was only spread to that much, was it an entitlement what a hell of a predicament some are having appointment after appointment just to get a disappointment, is this justifiable or am I just paranoid' maybe the brain is being beckon more by those who activate it more, we are not all the same height with the same foresight and will power to conquer' obstacles vary and vanity is a possibility, I know that if one sets out to do a little they end up doing a lot, and one who sets out to do a lot does a little' why is that I do not know but it seems to flow like a show, then that individual becomes the show, but it is not always for show' when you know it, it is for show, as you are the show. The power brain propels you to what you have to as it never sleeps, or weeps about fatigue having that inch sable appetite for continuous, not having to refocus as it is steady going with morning turning to evening and continuing' like a machine only to stop to reload. The machine age has been around in a different stage' look at this new brain wave that has taken us to another stage, welcome to the computer age mirrored after the mind or brain, we often paint them with the same brush' as we often get the same rush, one is visible and tangible the other is invisible and impossible' but they work in tandem creating this untouchable combination, a form ah double opponent that is always present' no form of accomplishment could be acquired without the mind involvement, even the brain is limited in that respect' as physical tangible and visible is at the mercy of invisible, it would be correct to surges that the mind could actually be the power source behind the brain' as the microcosm is encompassed by the macrocosm, so if one is enclosed by the other the enclose must be superior. The mind is so powerful it is divided into two realms conscious and unconscious, like life and what we call death. Matters of the heart emotions is controlled by the powerful mind, lifelong decisions are made from emotions humans and animals are controlled by emotions, although things go wrong sometimes love is love look at what happens in the name of love, opposites attract in the name of love. Same sex attract in the name of love, tugs fall in love in the name of love' immature loves the mature in the name of love, the things you do in love and for love is nothing like you would ever do if it wasn't for love' what is this weakness you inherit when in love, why does one become considerate and tolerate what they won't under different circumstances' how does one collapse and cave in like a house of cards under the influence of love. A tantalizing mind powering and over powering dominance of adherence That isn't visible or tangible that does not even seem feasible, but the feeling is unmistakable' how can an invisible feeling seem so real, it even seems like a feeling is on par with a seeing because if seeing is believing then a feeling is also a believing' if an individual is willing to risk everything on a feeling then that has to be something, it could be classified as stupidity personified or as nativity multiplied' when mind power is applied a millionaire will fall for a pauper and not even murmur, skin color and ethnicity doesn't even matter' a killer will be able to seduce a preachers daughter, lifelong family enemies for generations will be able to produce a collaboration' as negative and positive has proven to be power generating, it is all beyond me I have this inability to compute' like a cloud sailing high over my head, all I could do is allow it to sail away without a challenge' that is my portion. Our mind power cannot be contained or challenged, like preventing air from being any and everywhere on this earth' the mental capacity of the mind is mysterious and the envy of all focus, whatever needs to be accomplished the mind plays a part in it' like how money has a monopoly on the conscious, the mind has that kind of monopoly on the subconscious' only our mind power has the capacity to grant us the realization about Jesus, so it shouldn't seem far fetch to seek god realization from within because everything is within and everything comes from within, so if one does not seek the lord from within' they will be without, like most of us searching for Jesus or waiting for Jesus for two thousand years' the only way that concept floats my boat some kind of going and coming has to be taking place, because if my soul is the only thing I own in this hold wide world' everything else has been borrowed. So even my mind is not my own, it is on loan burrowed from someone else' no wonder it is so advance I don't even stand a chance to compete, that is why it dictates and disappears and leaves us to deal with all off our fears and insecurities' stability is an impossibility because it has no allegiance to anybody as everybody is on borrowed time, so there is no need to get to know anyone inside out' the mind power works on the permanent default mode. So everyone just fall in line and just do there time' as everything is for a time and is govern by an appointed time, as we are given a limited count our days are numbered on the mount' we cannot ask for a recount or add a count when our number is out we are out, so all this stuff is predestined so our experiences and interactions might not just be a matter of chance, this movie had a prewritten script with the actors being chosen beforehand. That is why nothing is in our hand and we don't have a free hand or a free will. As we plan out our life here, there is another plan already in place' so our efforts will have to go to waste ; it collides with the master plan and of course the master plan overrides our plan, as the mind overrides the brain because the mental overrides the physical every time' then we come down to the concept of the image, in this physical form the image controls the mirror image because without the image the mirror image cannot exist' so if the force of gravity reverses in space then the image and the mirror image could also have a reverse affect but that hasn't been proven to be true yet. The mind power pack we know is on a continuous attack, the brain of course makes an impact, but like us it doesn't have free will and it could be overturned at will' so until something changes which is not likely anytime soon, our mind will continue to rule the roost unchallenged like a dictator as that is the will of the master' we do not need to agree just agree to disagree. The game of role play continues, so it is absolutely necessary to accept your role and play on your pole, as the story is being told because it is a hand over and everything must be perfect over yonder, as this is being supervised by the manipulator mind power, speculations are in line for elations but do not hold your breath, you haven't been endorsed yet so don't fret. Worry not about what you can't do, think about what you can do' the mind power already dominates the pack, it is not smart to think about what you lack' in fact most of this is predestined anyway, almost everyone will not really have their way, it will be just role play' so just pace yourself to please yourself, do not ask any favors the mind power does no favors' everything is done by the book, visible defaults walks you through the book, the script is prearranged and it cannot be rearranged' one minute more cannot be added or subtracted, so do not even think of lamenting or contemplating. From resourcing for this project information was endless, even my taught process was influence by my mind power' producing a lot of fire with the heat rolling over, a lot of what came out was just hanging out which I incorporated as part of the wording. At times I was confronted with the inability to think independently, but it was just temporary fortunately. When it comes down to the disruption of beliefs that has been UN gowning as an individual' logic is pivotal you do not always have to get physical, some things resonate so they gain more attention on a regular basis. As we all seek god realization but we want to do it on our terms, if we do not seek the help of our own mind' we will probably be wasting our time. As only a dweller in the subconscious could open us up to it. Understanding the subconscious and gaining god realization is magical, so any help from the mind is critical. But we revere the brain more as it is physical with that tangible connection, we still prefer the out- in as opposed to the in- in, as going in seems so unrealistic isn't it, so we can only begin understand the force if he she or it permits us. So we cannot even say for sure that we are serving the lord because of constant illusion, once spirituality comes into play. Who is to say we might be playing a fools game.

It might be difficult to tell someone with nothing that they need nothing and it is impossible to tell someone with everything that they don't need something else. They would think you are full of yourself and something just hit me. Is money more important to the rich or the poor is anybody sure' each one could answer for sure. Furthermore would the rich benefit more are you sure, the poor have needs but the rich are needy to, whose needs are more critical in this virtual universal' to each there own. I beg to differ; justification is based on what indication. Is it on a pee-tee party or on one of those wealthy parties, at the end of the day' what could you say. Is it observation, to be given authentication, is it longing or craving or maybe plain old wanting. The squeaky wheel gets the grease because attention was brought to it, what about suffering in silence is that important or unimportant, acknowledgement could be given to the known, what about the unknown' the lord has done so much for me half of what is unknown to me I hope he never forgets me. The elite have it wrapped up like a mummy and I continue to feel worry. I lack money and everything takes money, living and also dying relates to money. My disappointment of me having less money has given me an appointment with acknowledgment and endorsement. Being a have not does not mean I should or would have not. Frugality with money definitely helps you and me to face reality. You should not spend what you didn't earn that is something you just have to learn, adjustments makes statement to keep you in agreement. No pain is no gain and time spent is time went. Preparation is the law of that I am sure, when you are prepared you have no fear even if fear is there your taught will be elsewhere. Like on the dream, you need a dream because, without a dream it is easy to sweep you off your feet. Beginning any dream could be risky like false history. But you stay the course of course, you have no recourse, to understand the course, you need to ride the horse. Anyone could cry good try, but you will only get teary eyed, you need to be wide open eye, if your try is going to be worthwhile. Obstacles hit like a brick, so your skull got to be thick, you must be prepare to take a licking. So if it comes you are prepared for the coming. But when it comes to the lord, not many are prepared for the coming' as everyone is scared of dying. Take a hit and fake a hit, bluffing is good for something, sometimes you have to call your bluff you are now equal when it becomes a ritual, practice falling so when you fall it will not phase you at all. It is time to get it on, courage under fire averts disaster. Pretense has consequences, remember to not settle yourself and get too comfortable. In case your nemesis should step up, the reason will be to take you out. If prepared you will not lose your head and become sightless. We learn when we are right and we learn when we are wrong. Through it all we learn more when we go wrong, but we are fixated on being right, as we are taught to be right, in the light of being right, I guess that is all right. Reality dictates and never hesitates, truth is a realistic pill. You cannot fool yourself even if you try, would you try just to satisfy a hunch, you cannot hide from yourself, even if you close your eyes and cannot see yourself, you would still be conscious of your living self. Because you learn as you go the learning comes as you go. If you get stagnant or dormant you become absent. life lessons are real lessons sometimes you gr-eave sometimes you feel as if you get touched though, you on your way to go, that touch is like major it is a door opener to the inner stuff. When a sinner get to experience that outer stuff, we think that is enough. Realization knows that you know, and you could explain to someone why it is so, it's a belief structure driven by confidence which has a major consequence. Self-realization precedes god realization only when you have found yourself could you find your god self. If you don't know what you are capable of would you believe what God is capable of God implores us to do one thing above each and everything, it is not only humans but animals too, just try it is why we live, just try you could even be still, it will be good for you when you try, when we learn how that's how we get to know how, not trying will limit your know how. You cannot accelerate if you are tipping the brake, as we run the race. This marathon called life will change what happen in our lives, places will change and faces will change at different stages. Even our lead will change, so we got to give and take, it's a game of high stakes each one must teach one, that goes for everyone, some think they are better, realization begs to differ. There is never an identical scenario, so who is to know what they don't know, after the fact is good but before the fact is always better. Help at random and work in tandem there is never a good time to do anything or to try anything but don't do nothing, just try something. Good things await the trier; they are always in the running to be hired. The name has changed but the game continues to be the same, it's now innovator a new outlook on an old in look, the trier is the author of such a book I am connected hook line and sinker. With money being the dunker, without the money it will be a sinker. I will have no power, we will have no power, money is the driver I am just the rider, the mirror image goes with the image, the reflection is void of intention I am not even certain to be a survivor, with every decision to be made money will be the final save, if there are restraint or constraints, money saves the day. If I concoct a cool idea, only money could take it further, so if I don't have a little something nothing doing, that's demoralizing. To bridge and full any gap for a fact, money is the thing to do that. The money act is the leader of the pact, it is never cumbersome that is awesome. Something like that will invigorate any situation. Its flexibility is acceptable that's no trouble; with that kind of status no wonder it is a major focus, when money is present that in itself is a present. When money disappears or is dormant that happens in a flash, that dominant machine brings everything to its knees like a cold freeze. Money is the save and it treats us all like its slave, some of us cave, as we try to pave our way each and every day, the fight is in the bight. You could chew the contents of your bite, chew it right and you win the fight. We learn gradually and we earn gradually, we breathe gradually and we achieve gradually, so belief should come gradually because relief is going to come gradually. Like realization belief gives you a huge relief. Positive is never destructive and it is your prerogative, weather you want to be attentive or even sensitive, it is informative though and always helpful when you know. Money is time and time is money, if you have time you could have money because it takes time to make money that makes everybody uneasy. That's why some fall for the quick fix, a quick entrance and a quick exit like the bee syndrome pollinating quick. It is understandable wanting without much trouble, but you get out what you put in, that's old school the original rule sacrifice, not nice if you in for the heist, a taker will just take with a straight face and take again and again. A giver will always give if they have to give, in our system today you take what you get and what you get you are being trained to be selfish and even ruthless. Some will take all that you have and keep all that they have and wouldn't even budge or give it a second taught, I guess ones conscience is flexible and manageable. Turning a blind eye is becoming easy to come by, with practice anything could become perfect Some kids don't share I wonder if their parents did, some adults don't share I guess it isn't rear, so what if I care. The journey is the destination and the destination is the journey, when you get there who cares, reaching there was more than hot air, we remember moments that's potent, giving us confidence. A good influence is like a good consequence, all is good that is good. Mountains are made from mole hills, so you could conquer a mole hill before a mountain. Small steps are designed to be positive to remove the doubts created by negative taught Baby steps seems to be perfect steps, as we get older we want to widen our steps. But our try steps are still baby steps anything you start in life takes baby steps, anything you think in life take baby steps, anything you dream in life is a baby step. The startup of anything is a baby step that is why a child could lead us realistically, experience is a good teacher but innovation is the principal the principle is thinking outside the box, bringing new ways to do old stuff. That will keep you out of the box and that in itself is a plus. Confinement isn't refinement it could create an assortment like procurement, the principle of simplicity is easy. Among the complicated it is relegated although tolerated, its mystified as you read through the lines and the money comes with conditions like love and seduction. Money could make a common breed a special breed. Superficial as it may seem to be, we could agree to disagree, money changes your lane and your game it does not matter what you into or if you are well to do, things come to you. I guess money brings them to you. When you have money you could afford to live and afford to die. Obstacles are just particles, the rich go by like a fly, money could make you and also break you, and it could dominate you and incriminate you, as you try to make a better you. Maybe a more comfortable you is always a realistic possibility if you persevere naturally.

Faces and places will change around you, some will be left behind most likely will take it unkind, as you explore your upward climb every time. You are dammed if you do and you are dammed if you don't. If you won't you on your own, dealing with the unknown is well known you are not expected to be known, a no show will be expected but if you show up then you did not flop. If you don't respect money you are living a folly, so you will always be melon coly, not the place to be, there is always more than what meets the eye, sometimes you don't see what is right in your eyes. Only realization could enlighten you, like your animal instinct, it hits you like magic, then you feel like magic' realizing somethings we might think are unrealistic ends up being so real' by having a real feel. Money makes the rules and also the news, when you don't have money you abide by the rules. The system dictates, get money or you are going contrary, get money to make life easy because the system wants it's bit from your little bit. Don't you ever forget it if you don't have anything to give the system does not care if you live You must have to rule so a have not cannot rule to call a shot you must have a shot, if you don't that was your shot. A ruler is a controller drunk or sober the owner of the dollar always gives the order. This side is mine that side is thine. As long as you don't cross over things will be fine. I could do yours but you cannot do mines a sucker gets played continuously like monopoly. One see what they want to see being oblivious could or could not be obvious what is on your plate usually determines how you play. I am dumfounded by what money can do it is real as can be to me. To use a chess analogy for clarification and simplification, I am the rook or even the pawn in the game enduring pain again and again. Money is king and queen if you know what I mean providing meals and making dreams a reality. It seems money is synonym with mobility, no money is just a travesty and disability, sometimes I think money avoids me like the plague. Incarcerated in a cage at every stage, to have it I must go get it so to count on it I have to key it in. Unlocked I have no luck; I could count on it only if it is locked in, then it does the trick and gives me my fix. There is no substitute to the money kit, it does tricks and it even has wings. It will fly away if it is not locked away, you cannot trust it to stay anyway. It is attracted to more money like birds of a feather it flocks together. Money could be a pleasure although a temporary pleasure, realistic and sadistic are other ways to describe it. Some go ballistic over it I guess it is what it is one major thought it is a legitimate monopoly that isn't a folly. To get ahead you need it, if you don't have it forget it, having it keeps you alive with pride and rejuvenated inside, it has the power to enhance your natural smile and it is healthy to have some. With some you will be welcome, it will always be your guide, if it is staying away continuously, it is no mystery your game needs a little tweaking, to convince it about staying. If there is more to be made it will be in the game over and over again it gets lonesome being the only some, knowing that has the potential to be awesome. Money works best in an investment test, keeping it to close to your chest is actually useless Being good and bad it keeps you on your toes, juggling could be troubling when you don't know what you are wanting. If you learn your craft at least in part before you start. Then the try will be worth it when you have something to show for it. Everything is temporary like your money and your memory. Cherish it while you have it because one day you might not have it, use it like you could lose it, one day you might not have it. There have been many with plenty and currently they don't have any. Some even won the lottery few years later they falter, but poverty accepts anybody, it is only supposed to be temporary, it is a launching pad as you tinker with your game plan. Roll over and do your make over, because it isn't over till it is over a smile is a frown turned upside down. Money could keep that smile year round. Nobody is giving away money so we must find a way to make money stay. It is up to yourself to motivate yourself, bluff yourself to sight yourself keep this quiet, you don't have to cause a riot, repeat it enough till your belief comes, it is tough work your belief is your relief. If you believe the same you could achieve the same, silence is golden while you wobble in trouble excitement in silence is a personal endorsement. I can do it do it I know I can do it, if you repeat it repeat it repeat it in time you will believe it because we believe what we hare that's crystal clear. Sometimes it is unfair the truth is not always what we here but we believe it I swear. A bate gives access to the taste why not give your own self a taste, because a taste is a taste, make haste and don't let it waste. The mind is awesome like that, you could tinker with stuff just like that you lead it will follow, it could be sometimes shallow. Time is older than respect and honor, so time should always be honored, if you have time you are alive, if you out of time by bye. We say enough is enough but we can never get enough, while some are expanding others are contracting. It goes without saying, take a chance on something, take a chance on someone make yourself that someone. If you do not take a chance you will lose your chance, you are your only chance to enhance your existence Reach out and try out or later you may be crying out because time is out. The limit is basically nothing more will fit no room to move even if you disapprove you cannot improve. I guess society created that proverbial box or idiom. Which is now a go to phrase; It is society way of labeling me as it contemplates on me. Fox holing me is trying to control me, but like air confining me to my little space will not limit me to handle me. The floods gates are washed away per say, I am sailing away on my terms and in my way, raft riding first class. To differentiate me from other starts, I cannot be taken apart. I was never made up, because I showed up here does not mean I am stuck here. What brings could carry, money brings so it would carry harmony to families worldwide. But there is a kicker here is where things differ, financial bliss is not a myth. But to continuously expect it is a mistake, when the system of manipulation is in operation it deviates and permeates as it makes its escape' we loves to contain money, but it always loves to be free as every human loves freedom' they are unable to give their money that same freedom. Everything in the game never stays the same, on the other hand manipulation demands what it can when it can, what you earn is not yours alone there is a hand out turning your pockets inside out. That's the fall out, life is fragile you must be agile, when there is no money it helps no body, anything you want to do will be futile. You feel like a rejected feline, there is no spring in your steps, your face is now visibly upset, out of sight is out of mind, and it is like that most times. Easy becomes difficult when visibility is called into account. You do not respect what you do not see, that is why the concept of the lord is a may be. With endless possibilities that just confuses it for us. We are hoping for heaven but cannot imagine dying, obsess with the body, our earthly spectacle which is a temporary receptacle, that is just recyclable, blinding us and deceiving us, because some of us think we are the focus, their isn't nothing more ludicrous. There goes the mind again going along with the deceiving game simple belief is temporary until realization arrive putting doubts into oblivion. Fiction is a depiction of some ones imagination, is not dreaming someone imagination, or did I come to the wrong conclusion, I guess it is my imagination, it is an action never the less. You might think that it is far fetch. It is close like a finger from another finger Everything is connected So any action could cause a chain reaction As I see it money is cede and it is never free, it is only about money it has always been about money it will always be about money anyone who say it is not about money already have money. So to then it wills defiantly it is so reel to me now it is clear as natural air. This domination have spiritual proportions, although we have to leave it all here, the churches insist it will help to get you up there somewhere. It is kind of unfair and unclear by insinuating Money is the target like the Scottish loving haggish, even the preacher is on the money run, the teacher is on the money run, of course the lawyer is on the money run and it goes on and on. No wonder why we delicate our entire working life towards earning money, someone somewhere is always after money only god could save us from money because god alone does not need money. Is it not ironic we need money at least that's what we are told to be able to save our own soul they demand ten percent total nonsense So you must keep working and scrambling to have affiliations with the lord because the church stuff seems like a bluff about the lord. That is tough so it is a business like any business your business is to mind your business and get money to handle your business. This delusion is far and wide mister illusion has us running wild we are petrified and disorganized as we take a scuba dive free falling all the while. We are actually mummified alive only god could save us on this ride the irony is it is mass confusion hidden delusion. We are fools rushing in where wise ones fare to go our destruction is certain because we are uncertain. Nothing is clear until realization gets us there. That's why manipulation has us in a choke hold; all that's important is inhaling and exhaling. Money has us so corrupt everything we do is so abrupt. Not caring not loving not contemplating on the important things like a kind word or simple smile that could carry us along on our ride. Stuff could be intense, should we be so tense, leaning on the fence might make some real sense. Repeating the same old is getting to old, being boxed in is too confining Interpretation could be confrontational; it is often a bridge to disruption.

Then the destruction comes; how you see stuff could clear up stuff. How you hear could make things so clear and you're aware your action is your works. That's why your action speaks louder than your words. If you mean it when you say it, only when you keep it you acknowledge it. Then it becomes full proof some ones word used to be there bond, now it is something that you throw into the pond and run from. Misrepresentation of one self is a fictionalization of one self, sometimes used for deceit in a situation. Starting off wrong always lead you wrong, but right and wrong could coexist like positive and negative. Because of the actuality that one needs the other to be effective. Why it is like that for the life of me I don't get that, I guess no one is perfect. Does it mean only god could be all positive because his power is affirmative. The deeper you go it does not get easier though in every good person is bad person, that's why life is uncertain. Whatever you harbor could actually inspire, motivation comes when benefit comes a compromise could tantalize as you try to analyze. Worldwide combinations work in tandem to create cohesion. There is a time and place for everything, a time to try something and a time to do nothing, because there has to be a time for some observing. There is a reason why change is constant because goodness is not always present' to implore a financial phrase a correction is needed for balance. Adjustments transform life this surely is a hell of a life, but you only benefit when you contribute to life; even if you are not yet ready' life is ready for you, as we are just tools to help shape and for good. Where there is truth a lie is close by, the cover up is done by infecting the truth with a little white lie; a little black lie is not acceptable in that receptacle Sometime truth hurt that Is why we continue to work on little things. To create interest in the bigger things that is reusable and valuable when stuff becomes disposable. Then we get in trouble because what you dispose of always seems to be the wrong stuff and must be recouped. Therein lies the proof, if you do not have the skill set' you will get upset, continuity helps the domination component; it holds the key to continuity. Having it means getting something continuously available; therein lies the fable, not much is continuous. The personal guarantee money does that so easily. That commodity is everybody easy pill under the sill' it will sued any chill Being number one is only that could be lonely, combinations are popular and you stand to go further with the prop factor. One depends on the other; things are made much easier with help and self-help creating that mesh and confidence in one self, good for a while only for a little while until expansion changes the tide. By that time you will be ready for the addition on extending your help along. Rejuvenation in motion is a deserving action; it is energized If the church creates belief that could be a relief, being relevant is convenient that makes sense. Any help is good I would help if I could, but if you say in order to get help I must pay for help because the lord needs my help. Heaven is free there isn't a fee, deluding me will not set you free. God is truth so tell me the truth do not use money as a deceiving fruit. Emotions are vulnerable don't use me as a bundle because I stumble and fumble I am also humble don't confuse me to manipulate me. Believing fictitious rubble is trouble from the get go, someone who believe is innocent until proven guilty scholars believed the earth was flat for centuries then they were proven wrong. God want my time not my tide to tidy up my inside, without money a human diminishes without money our lord flourishes. Where money is concerned to the lord it is of no concern because money is earthly the lord is heavenly. What is needed greatly on this earthly realm is of no consequence on the spiritual realm; earthly enrichment ends in disappointment. There is a reason why riches do not get you to heaven. And there is no monopoly that pulls you to the lord. Status is hopeless like endless success on earth is useless, maybe got to be simplicity is the exception, but that's only a perception. Water and oil do not mix one will rise above and one will stay below. Spiritual and carnal is part of that faction that is why there are so many interpretations consideration should be given throughout the duration. Each individual will have their own opinion at the end of the day. Heaven holds a place for those who pray with hope. It is an in in, but we think it is an out in' but substance flows from within. Suddenly that disposable commodity money that makes us disposable becomes disposable. What do you know because you know you in trouble when you do not have money on earth all things possible become obsolete and discrete? The big high becomes a big slide when positions are reversed. Because love is about money and war is about money that is an earthly folly that follows us continuously, in reality it is borderline truthful as when you have no money everything is about making money. Like a smile is a frown turned upside down, love is war turned upside down; and when you read love backwards it is e vol. When money isn't around, everything is turned upside down, so we are stuck in the wroth that disables most of us, then things start to fester sooner or later it is sure disaster. Some of us admit to being unable and we throw in the towel. Only a low percentage of us are the fighters, as many are just settlers. The rest will probably surrender the top ten percent controls the bulk of the wealth the bottom percentage is at a disadvantage. So money is about control and who got the money will control, domination is control the domination imposes power that is why it causes so much disaster. A taker isn't a giver that is fuel for retaliation, as long as domination is the major option the presence of war will not go on vacation. We will continue to have war on stay cation because the ten percent rule means domination. Many more will have to suffer, many more will have to die, as realization steps in line we will continue to ask why, tell me why as we continue to seek our piece of the pie. Where there is life there will be hope, that thing called hope isn't no joke, it could be self-administered which makes it feasible and it is surely durable, once it is in place, it has a base which works like faith. When what was given was depleted, it somehow has to be repeated, that's why it is so important and potent, and for every action there is a reaction. Every situation has an occasion because the process is continuous. Relevance will be the focus, what may have been relevant in past times may not be relevant this time. The more things change the more they remain the same. A different outlook does not mean a different in look, what you see when you look all depends on how you look. Someone mind is a major influence, it is the player in the life game, you know it is a game right, a game of survival. There is always a rival to cause a reprisal, someone will not agree with your opinion, so it is ongoing and endless. A sprinter cannot be a good adviser in a marathon and expect to be effective that is logical. If one is broke they cannot be expected to advise on finances, simple logic so what will you say is the rule, that would help if it helps someone to improve. Trying is what comes to mind, every time it helps, it helps every time. When you try and it works, right away you realize this isn't a joke. So why do not many more try, there is an underlying lying current called fear, of the unknown, it is sometimes unclear but what is clear, it stalls you like a statue and makes you lifeless like a statue, then you per-sue nothing. Most really fear it could be intimidating because fear remains there is a mist. In the air it exists to scare, if you fear, you just remain right where you are and you remain what you are. That is clear fear is a retardant so it treats you like a retard. You will not take a chance, that is not who you are, so far adjustments makes a wealth of a difference. Trying is an achievement in a nut shell, you need it to learn any skill you need it to earn your money that is pleasing to anybody. The covering could disguise and misrepresent the inside. The cover story is not the real story, when you open up the flavor is served up then you are covered up. Someone must sacrifice something in order to gain something, because you get out what you put in. That is so interesting, it is magical, some try to get something out without putting out anything that is a fall out, some prefer a hand out, and not a try out that way they are not obligated to put out. Nothing ventured means nothing gained, your game will remain the same, statue like looking lifeless. Same old soon becomes too old, innovative destroys out dated and stagnant is certainly dormant Mobility have the ability of visibility you move freely when you could see clearly, a visionary have the ability of insight, that's the guide for doing it right I would say though, right or wrong is a move you learn from, a right or a wrong move keeps you in tune, no move is not a good move you improve when you move, circulation improves. Money keeps you on the move, you will not be sulking. You will be thinking of something, you will be upbeat and your adrenalin will be flowing, so dormancy won't exist because mobility defeated it. Physically and mentally you are ready to conquer, which is the armor of the conqueror, the conquer in this case is the commodity money The domination exerts power and rules all over because of the acquisition factor, a durable useable tool a main stay that possesses like an evil spirit. Domination is an occupation that dominates like an evil spirit, merciless and careless regardless of status Greed dominates need that's why the needy is ignored by the greedy, being a have not means society cares not, if you have nothing to give society does not care if you live, as society is just waiting for a piece of your pie' if you cannot deliver you will get the cold shoulder. Only God cares if you live or not, only god cares if you exist or not. The difference between God and money are conditions, God love you and I without conditions, another human will love you but there is always conditions. If you are broke not much will work, because you are getting choked trying to get things to work, it sounds like a joke don't it. Only God cares about you before you have made it. Everybody cares about you because you made it, but it is superficial and equivocal. Nobody cares about you that are why you are a no body. So everybody could actually care, if there is a dare, I think I am being fare The trick is to be needed, money is always needed, then you get respected and represented, there is something about being wanted. That is when you stand predominant regardless of existing opinions finding and knowing your skill set is designed to get you set, finding yourself is not easy but you could find yourself somewhat easily. Knowing what works or what you lucky with, will give you some comfort you feel legit. Challenge yourself when you do not have to, avoid settling if you do not fit in, time will guide you in the interim, ultimately time chooses for you when you do not choose for you. There is a window a temporary window, that opens for you, as time goes on life goes on then the window closes gradually. Things happen and the blinkers goes on like blinders they keep your focus. We sometimes stumble, on something interesting to us.

Just like that we are living our dream; the big bang concept serves some purpose after all. Life is a marathon not a sprint, what impacted in the beginning stays with you to the end There are consequences for every action and a reaction to an action some call it contemplation. Some call it inseparable oneness on this earthly realm separation from money is a no can do. On the spiritual realm separation from God is a no can do. What do we do, the best we can do, is what a clear conscience implore us to do by representing ourselves in whatever we do. I got a notion on this occasion, that's destined to cause some confusion. Is money synonymous with the world famous mark of the beast, if you will not be able to purchase anything without the mark and you will be left in the dark, am I paranoid or plain old annoyed As I am confronted with a dominant message, I am being squished like a sausage in a sandwich. Money is stifling me to stillness, I am trying to get it on, but money is bent on making it wrong. Because I was born without a crown does not mean I was destined to be down. Money could be described as selfish, it could also make you selfish, I guess after not having it, I think I could get the fact of one wanting to keep it in tact. Once you get it, you will probably guard it, easily understandable without even a mumble, to impose on it, money gives you authority because it possesses authority, you could gain the whole world though but still lose your soul. You do not want that though, your soul is all you got in your bag pack. Your soul is you, even if you do not know that for a fact, it is truly you. Your soul knows you like your name it is the one thing that is exclusive to us. That is how karma follows you weather you know it or not, you have to settle your account, hell we have to settle our account. Some say karma do not count, you live once and you die once, so what is the reasoning behind forgiving our sinning, what is sinning isn't it our doing. What is karma isn't it also our doing, so if we did whatever then we should be responsible for whatever, there is no free ride in any life, it is easier to commit and harder to remit But I keep hearing preachers say, ask for your forgiveness and be a witness do not worry the lord will forgive any and every sin. Because he died for our sins, but we keep on sinning, will he keep on dying if we are not trying We use ten percent of our brain capacity, but still believe we could get off on a technicality, God is loving not stupid and he operates at full capacity daily, so if we are using just ten percent and the lord is at one hundred percent we cannot pull a wool over Gods eyes, even if we try so I wonder why we try. Saying you sorry, is it that easy, to dispose of unwanted sins, isn't that nice. Is it now easier to depose of sins than to commit them Money is being used as a tool to remit them. So money is playing us physically, now it is making a play for us spiritually. The dominance continues, money has a hold on the churches I'm told. In the first place, the lord made everything that was made in six days or six years and he rested on the seventh day, that's what they say but someone is being born every day and someone dies every day and the soul do not dwell with the dead oh well. I do not know more for sure so let's close that door. Money is the kingpin, of use everywhere it is plausible and applicable, Accountability poses no trouble, accompaniment is the action of success, association with money is envious, that is obvious, it activates on having visibility of the subject, ones inner taught could make then a convict, the crime of not having is draining from what is remaining, money now have earthly domination, to our lord it is just earthly destruction, because all the money stays here when we exit, from here on, anything that money could buy would be left like items on a drive by. Money is like words you communicate with, with, money that should be the end of the story. Currently we dictate with money, we dictate because of money, our entire lives is centered around money, some say God want us to prosper, even if it is on the backs of a brother or sister, but thanks to God there is a time period for everything, and change is continuously happening So hope is contagious while called Christians have been banking on hope for centuries, on the returning of the lord, what happened before and after the lord, who was the focus, off course nobody actually knows the lord, so he could already be here, no one alive could connect, there we could all be sleep like, walking zombies in the making, unaware of our surroundings. What in the world is even happening, this life is fragile like a dream and nothing is ever like what it seems. It is a worldwide assumption and off course, there is no manual it is trial. And it is an error situation emphasizing trying, the key to learning and experiencing anything. Money is the earthly king, trying is the earthly queen, once you try you could achieve far and wide, that is a combination of success. Independence will build your confidence, money is all right but the lord is right by all, to the lord money is just another insignificant option while to us human's money is the real option. In accepted reality the world is in threefold, you have the first world the world of the haves, the second world the world of those who think they have, then we have the third world, the world of the have not, our existing triangle r concept. Which is self-explanatory the three sides must be connected to be effective, if the concept is not triangulated, it is destined to fail, so believe it or not, the rich needs the poor and the poor needs the rich, with the variable being fairness, a livable wage for honest work anytime that is compromised. The triangulation becomes undone, so although money is king it needs the work to be done, in order for the domination to continue, desperation is always a deterrent that creates a smoke screen to hinder visibility and clarity. So when we do not see clearly, agreement is in jeopardy, when that happens the order of business becomes a nightmare of business, one side usually compromises, to impede continuity. Money is the jell that makes things work so well, on earth each sphere has its wonder, solar power is another wonder from over yonder, water and fresh air is invaluable hear on earth, humans are here just to try to make it back, to their original home, this is the playing ground, look at how money plays us around, you know because this life is a game, a game of survival and revival. Where we are playing roles, as we stroll towards our real goal, finding ourselves and knowing ourselves, then finding our lord and savior, and contemplating on him, everything comes from him, so even a steer from him could make a world of a difference, in reference to wisdom knowledge and pure understanding. So we will not have to be guessing and be consumed by illusion, who are bent on using tricks, someone mind Is vulnerable, as it is flexible to creativity, the mind is imaginative, and it is open to superlatives and comparatives, that's why innovative is massive, it has a built in advantage, because it creates a brand new package, innovation is like creation, the adaption of a notion, to give it traction, and to get participation, you need advertisement, so the money is crucial for arrival and survival. To bridge the gap and to pull the slack; creating a real impact. When a crack needs to be filled, you already know the drill; I admit money pleases me like I know it pleases you. What am I going to do if there is no money, twiddle my thumb pretend I am dumb, look at time run like a rerun, when there is money everybody is happy, you have mobility and possibility, Working together in perfect harmony, there is no animosity or inscrutability. The accountability is, money answers to nobody, because nobody is bigger than money, we devote our entire working lives, in a quest for earning money, So don't tell me it is not about money, it is only about money, to do things well and to jell, even to feel good like well, keep money in your head, when your taught is money, you cannot help but to feel wealthy, a feeling is important, it makes a good assistant, it helps to guide and drive, while you venture and prosper, faith paid off it is a light, that we sometimes turn off, it is designed to keep us humble, it is only natural for us to stumble, and for us to know it is alright to be not right, that teaches us we need to fight to make things alright, fighting is not necessary brawling, it is a strategy that helps in different capacities. Seize matters for verbalizing, it is exciting, that is all it is, only effective use of what you got, could get you what you really want, the fight is in the dog, not in the seize of the dog, that is where a lot of us go wrong. Life could be a run around, as we try to find our way around, the variable is money, we do everything for the money, that's why the domination is easy, who controls the money controls everybody, the mark of the beast have to be money, what else could control everybody, that's why it is so easy, for Lucifer to devour us, it is like taking candy from a baby, no if or maybe, when you know what somebody wants, you could give them what they want, who give it could take it away any day, per say. With the lord being the word and all that, there is no color to a word or nationality like that. Just reality is always present in simplicity in a word, everyone needs the word and everyone could use words' for expression and satisfaction to bring about normalization. Some go for sophistication, to get satisfaction, the word is the action, why God is great, he could relate, truth always takes the cake, the truth could hurt, the truth could choke, it could work and it could work well, because we are looking for instant results, that's how we go wrong, our word is to give and to keep, that's why the word is so deep. There is not much you could give and still keep. that is the way so anyone could have their own way, the word always lead us as we speak; it always precedes us where did all this complication come from, the word belongs to everybody, anybody has autonomy, no one owns the word really, but everyone is bound by the word, it was it is it is what it is, the word is all there is, because the word is the lord of host, you could explain anything with the word, you could say anything with a word. Simplification personified is the word you could live by, you will know someone by their words, and people tend to or try to exploit the word. So do not try to confuse the word, to break your word, although it is imaginary, you know what is customary, the word is so powerful it could be positive and negative, a two edged sword that cuts both ways, the user is articulatory and divert-err. The word is free like heaven is free, humans got interested and introduced a fee, so money is for human, only money pleases a human, if nothing else is going right and there is money, a human could be happy, there is no love without money, there is no power without money, there is no activity without money, so money is mobility, and accountability to money, is the ability to use it wisely, a fool and there money is always apart. Money has a strategy to always depart' that is the message it wants to impart Money is a bridge to the ridge, climbing that hill would need some will, when there seems to be no way, your will is the way to find your way, to be pleasing that's a given, when you could articulate you could translate, if anything is out of range, breaking it down is the word game, silence is so golden that's why the word is the chosen, the word never speaks, and our interpretation is so weak, one tenth is the consent we give, it is at our disposal at will, we are pretending to know what we don't know, risking personal crucifixion which is an addiction, as money is already an addiction, it is just birds of a feather flying together, we stupefy ourselves daily making a mockery of the worthy. The word could full us up, but our cup is over turned. And our hands are always open for money, oh lord I could surely use some more money, the word is the lords and the fullness there of, when we mix spiritual and carnal the resultant will be bacchanal. God is what God is, we all guess who god is, if God is the word, he is the world. He could be found all over the world, he is closer than a brother or a sister, but still we cannot find the lord, with all this intellect we are not willing to take risks, being circumspect we are scared of dying and you know I am not lie in. That's why an intellectual is a casualty to the facility, they will not admit but rather permit uneasiness, the nature of which is well known, money is the tool of this entire world, to make it you cannot do it without it like those before us. The rich was always the focus, some still want to take the wealth, old habits are still felt, we all die and some cry why, did you have to leave cut and dry, the movie was but for a few minutes, so the parts being acted would be for a few minutes, a minute of fame is what most tend to aim at, but most don't even get that, but the word is down pact, your exit is determined before your entrance is dawning, you cannot cheat your karma, it is you no need to bother. It is the contributing factor, for repeating this over and over. We are coming and going like time, always running to something, what to where to no one can tell you, may be the running is to the money, more lix is in the mix, as you make up the stagger, money leaps even further, money cares not about you or me, it is just passing through being expendable, making us vulnerable, it makes you temporarily comfortable, like a drug, then you want more, the chase becomes continuous, and you lose focus, you become a zombie, that's troubling to anybody. When the word makes you, it is solid standing and you will not be shaky. You could not be blown away easily, but when money makes you and it goes away, you crash and you look like trash, because you feel like trash. It is from the bottom up, steady as a rock, the maker is not a faker, trusting takes some waiting, these days we wanting what we are wanting, sooner is better, from our standpoint, later is greater from the lords standpoint. We trust less and we hope less, so we become hopeless and worthlessness. Hopelessness is uselessness, when you become like this it is a sickness, hope is no joke, that thing really works, it is a bridge to nowhere, when you get there you become aware, around the bend isn't the end, but this is the end thank you till we meet again. I love what I can do with money I do not like what money could do to me. It is a payoff, that makes most showoff, then it is difficult to get off, your dependency is your redundancy, and you end up its casualty. If you give a cookie to a monster, it will shake you down for some milk. You negotiate with money, but you do not risk your life on money. Use it as a tool that is the golden rule' only a fool tries to break the rules. But if you allow it to rule you, then you will be ruled, money only abides by the money rule, who got the money always makes the rules' so they can break them; as they are not bound by them. That is why money rules' it is the go to rule, the mule of the lifting tool. It engages humans and machines working in unison' there is no better solvent to give that ultimate result, as it possess the flexibility to be effective in every community' what a commodity not replicable easily the cream of the crop always awaited unabated.